MARCO RUIZ

Ferrari

Illustrations by Marco Giardina

CRESCENT BOOKS
New York

In this poster book the tables
are designed so that if you want
you can frame them.
For the single ones cut along the dashed line,
whereas the twin tables
can be pulled out of the book
by cutting the binding thread.

This 1988 edition
published by Crescent Books,
distributed by Crown Publishers, Inc.,
225 Park Avenue South,
New York, New York 10003.

Created by ADRIANO ZANNINO
Editorial assistant SERENELLA GENOESE ZERBI
Editor: Maria Luisa Ficarra
Translated from the Italian by Ruth Taylor
Consultant Guido Staderini

ISBN 0-517-66807-6

Color separation SEBI s.r.l., Milan
Typesetting Tipocrom s.r.l., Rome

Printed and bound in Italy by SAGDOS S.p.A., Milan

THE MYTH
OF THE PRANCING HORSE

The attraction and prestige that the Maranello-built cars acquired through the successes and dramas of a long racing career not only became the very symbol of the racing world itself, but also of the spirit of an unceasing will to question and surpass the results already achieved. From this point of view, the myth of the Prancing Horse is inevitably linked to the image of Enzo Ferrari. Born in 1898, he invested in his company a tenacious and iron will to proceed along his chosen path, overcoming all obstacles. The result has been forty years of extraordinary cars and endeavors.

A great inspirer of ideas, with a wise knowledge of the human soul and an acute ability to recognize talent both in technicians and drivers, Enzo Ferrari's success has made up for an existence that has not been lacking in sad moments.

Initially a driver, then owner of the Modenese team of the same name which ran Alfa Romeo's racing activity from 1929 to 1938, in 1946 Enzo Ferrari began the third and most prestigious phase of his career, that of manufacturer. When he left Alfa Romeo, the Milanese company made him agree not to produce cars under his own name for a period of four years. Thus the Auto Avio Costruzioni came into being, its first car being the 815. This was a spider Sports whose chassis and engine were both built using Fiat material. The displacement of the 8-cylinder in-line engine was 1,496 cm^3, and the two that were built were both entered in the 1940 Mille Miglia race, which took place on a circuit that started and finished in Brescia, passing through Cremona and Mantua. One of these cars was driven by Alberto Ascari, who held the lead in his category for a long time before retiring due to the breakage of one of the timing belts.

The war resulted in a diminishing passion for racing and in 1943 the company was transferred from Modena to Maranello due to the government imposed industrial decentralization plan. There it produced hydraulic grinders for another year, before being seriously hit during the bombing raids. Once the war was over the company assumed the name Ferrari and in 1947, with the 125, began a long series of successful cars. We have tried to retrace the company's path, through the most important models, in the following pages. This journey lasted 40 years and resulted in an unrivaled racing career with the following astonishing results: a total of nine Formula One Driver's World Championships, eight Manufacturer's World Championships and FIA Manufacturer's Cups, 13 World Championships in the Sports-Prototype category with nine victories in the Le Mans 24-Hour, and eight in the Mille Miglia. At the end of the 1987 season, the red Maranello-built single-seaters had won 93 Formula One Grand Prix.

From an industrial point of view, Ferrari's earliest production phase was extremely limited and, from a technical point of view, was closely linked to the racing cars. At the beginning of the 1960s, the firm was transformed into a limited company under the name of S.E.F.A.C. Spa, and the normal series models began to assume a more independent existence. Production increased rapidly, never deviating from quantities still well below 1,000 cars annually. Things changed radically in 1969, with the agreement stipulated with Fiat, by which the Turin-based company assumed control of the production factories, leaving Enzo Ferrari to run the racing department. Great successes were scored by both sectors during the 1970s. Between 1969 and 1979, the production capacity increased from 928 cars to 2,221, with an export rate of over 80%, while the Manufacturer's World Championship, won by the 312 P in 1972, was followed by Niki Lauda's glorious Championship titles in 1975 and 1977, and by Scheckter's in 1979. Although the success of the Ferrari series cars has continued along this line of continuous development in the 1980s, as far as the racing cars are concerned, no further world titles have been added to those previously conquered, despite exhilarating periods such as the career of the unfortunate champion Gilles Villeneuve, or Alboreto's victories in 1985, or those of Berger in 1987.

THE GRAND TOURERS

Although Ferrari immediately realized the need to introduce cars that were suitable for road use, it is not possible to speak of real series production until the Sixties. In fact, each model was conceived essentially for racing, and the "civilized" versions derived from them were virtually built for a particular clientele which chose its own chassis, a more or less powerful engine and bodywork offered by the main Italian body-makers of the time. The continuous technical development of the cars, which was due to Enzo Ferrari's insatiable desire to surpass the already obtained results, meant that not one of the Grand Tourers belonging to the early period was truly the same as another. In fact, the fascination which these cars possessed perhaps lay in the very fact that they were unique and in their close relationship with the original versions that were glorified through their victories in the Mille Miglia or the Le Mans 24-Hour race.

A key to establishing whether the early Ferraris were meant for the racing track or the road lies in their chassis numbers which, according to company policy, were even as far as the Sports were concerned and uneven in the case of the Grand Tourers. However, this method of classification is not foolproof. The largest number of road cars produced in the early years of this activity, the 342 Americas, all had even chassis numbers. At the same time 39 250 GTOs, produced from 1962-1964, and created exclusively for racing, were registered solely with uneven numbers.

As for the designation of the GT models, in principle the number that corresponded to the engine displacement followed by an identification code or name (for example, 212 Inter) was generally used. However, this does not mean that other criteria were not adopted, such as that used to identify the Superamerica series (400 and 410) which was based on an estimate of the total displacement. In addition, the Dino series' code was the result of linking the total displacement with the number of cylinders (196 and 308).

The evolutionary line of the Ferrari roadsters was launched by a series of cars that, between 1948 and 1953, adopted the 60° 12-cylinder V engine designed by Gioachino Colombo in 1946. This engine had made its debut on a Grand Tourer in the 166 Inter of 1948. The layout of this car consisted of a chassis with an elliptic ladder frame on which numerous coupé and cabriolet bodyworks (designed by the principal stylists of the time) were mounted. The first to work closely with Ferrari was Touring, which covered numerous cars with its famous Superleggera (Superlight) aluminum structure fastened to a frame of thin steel tubes. Touring was followed by Vignale (whose designer at the time was Giovanni Michelotti), the Stabilimenti Farina, Ghia, and lastly Pininfarina, whose first work for the Maranello company was a 212 Inter cabriolet in 1952.

The level of craftsmanship which characterized Ferrari's earliest production is revealed by the total number of cars constructed. In 1947, these amounted to three, and increased to only 57 by 1953, although the line between the road models and the racers is demonstrated by the ninth place obtained in the 1953 Nürburgring 1,000-km race by an elegant cabriolet belonging to the Italian film director Roberto Rossellini.

This initial series already revealed some of the prerogatives that were to become typical of the company: an evolution based on a progressive increase in engine displacement and the application of new solutions only after they had been widely tested in races. It was logical therefore that Ferrari should also soon begin to exploit the engine that Aurelio Lampredi had designed in 1950, for the GTs too. This engine had been highly successful in the 3.3, 4.1 and, lastly, in the 4.5 liters Formula One and Sports cars. Once again a 12-cylinder V, it differed from Colombo's engine above all in the larger wheelbase between the cylinders and the fixed heads onto which the cylinder liners were screwed. The differences between the Sports and GT versions of the Lampredi engine were minimal, lying solely in the lubrication system, which was of the dry sump type in the racing cars. The first road version to be equipped with it was the 340 America. Although this car was provided with more "civilized" bodywork than racing versions of the same name, it retained some characteristics typical of the latter, such as the right-hand drive. At the same time of the 30 or so built between 1951 and 1952, only eight had an unmistakably road-going layout. The subsequent 342 America assumed a

layout aimed more for use as a Tourer. Its power was also slightly reduced creating greater elasticity. Moreover, a 4-speed synchronized gearbox and left-hand drive were also adopted. Only six were built, all of which were prepared with much attention to luxury.

In 1953, the 212 Inter and the 342 America were replaced by a single project, which gave rise to the 4.5-liter 375 America and the identical 250 Europa, which was also provided with a Lampredi 12-V engine with displacement reduced to 3 liters. The most widely produced versions of the 30 built were the elegant coupés created on the drawing-boards of Pininfarina, which was well on its way to becoming the Maranello company's official body-maker. With the subsequent 410 Superamericas, which replaced the 375 America, the original Lampredi engine's road career came to an end. In the subsequent 400 SA it was replaced by a new engine derived from the Colombo 12-V. This had been developed in the meantime with the 250 GT, a model to which the Ferrari mark owes much of its fame, as well as its development at an industrial level. In fact, during this model's lifespan (1954-1964), the company's annual production rose from 58 cars to 654. The last of the 250 GT series was the GT/L version (production began in 1962) with bodywork characterized by its rare harmony and constructed by Scaglietti from a Pininfarina design.

In 1964, a new chapter began with the 330 GT series. It was provided with an engine derived from the 400 SA with an identical displacement. At the same time the wheelbase between the cylinders was modified in order to improve the water circulation and place the head elements in the optimum position. Furthermore for the first time the old dynamo was replaced by an alternator. In 1966, the coupé and two-seater spider "330 GTC/GTS" versions appeared. Between 1967, and 1968, all the 330 models were replaced by the new versions of the similar 365. Of these, the GTC/GTS remained in production until 1970, while the GT 2+2 remained in production until 1971. The two-seater variants were not subsequently followed up, while in 1971, the 365 GT4 replaced the 2+2. This was followed by the 400 and the 412, in 1976, and 1985, respectively.

By the mid-1960s the two lines produced by Ferrari were well differentiated, consisting on the one hand of the powerful Grand Tourers, and on the other of the berlinettas and two-seater spiders with more sporty characteristics. As far as the latter were concerned, in 1964, the generational change between the 250 GT and the 275 GTB occurred, the latter being provided with an engine that was closely related to that of the 275 P and 250 Le Mans Sports-Prototypes. In addition an independent suspension on the rear axle with transaxle gearbox in block with the differential was adopted. With this model the conceptual demarcation between the Ferrari Grand Tourers and racing cars could be considered complete. Produced until 1968, the successful 275 found a worthy successor in the Daytona, the last Ferrari berlinetta to be equipped with a front engine.

In 1969, there was a fall in production in respect to the previous 12 months, with it settling to an annual rate of 619 cars. However, this was a particularly important year in the company's history in that Enzo Ferrari ceded 50% of its shares to Fiat. The Turin-based company thus assumed control of Ferrari industrial activity, while Enzo Ferrari himself managed the racing sector independently. Moreover, six years previously, the desire to give Ferrari financial security had led the company's founder to begin discussions with Ford. These were brusquely interrupted on the eve of the contractual signing. This breakdown was caused by Ferrari's hesitation to cede its sports activity to the American giant. This resulted in Ford's entry in Sports-Prototypes races, assumed solely to vindicate itself on the track.

In 1971, production passed the 1,200 mark, thanks also to the success of the new Dino series (introduced in 1968) with 6-cylinder engine mounted in the rear. This allowed for a considerable increase in the company's clientele. Subsequent milestones were the 2,221 cars produced in 1979, the 3,119 produced in 1975, and the 3,956 produced in 1987, with an export rate that remained in the region of 75%.

An important technical turning point occurred in 1973, with the marketing of the Berlinetta Boxer, the first 12-cylinder Ferrari with rear engine, which remained in production until the launching of the Testarossa in 1984.

Ferrari 212 Inter

166-195-212 INTER

The coupé Touring version of the 166 Inter of 1948.

In 1947-1948, Ferrari had already become aware of the need to build cars that were not only meant for racing, but which were also suitable for driving on the road. An initial production unit for Grand Tourers of this type was launched in 1948 with the 166 Inter. Structurally very similar to the MM racing version presented at the Turin Show that year, it differed in its less powerful engine and a slightly longer wheelbase. The chassis was an elliptic tubular ladder frame, while the front suspension consisted of wishbones with transverse leaf springs. In the rear there was a rigid axle with longitudinal semi-elliptic leaf springs. Hydraulic lever dampers were installed. The engine adopted was the 1,995 cm³ 12-V designed by Gioachino Colombo. This version possessed single twin barrel carburetor feed capable of developing 115 hp at 6,000 rpm. This car, which had a five speed gearbox, reached maximum speed of about 93 mph (150 km/h). Several cars were nevertheless fitted with a three carburetor engine, with 140 hp at 6,600 rpm.

The first 166 Inters were fitted with bodywork designed by Touring, which built 21 almost identical coupés in the course of 1949. Another nine coupés were built by Vignale, as well as one by Ghia, while the Farina factory produced three cabriolets and four coupés. A closed version was also produced by Bertone.

In 1950, the 2-liter engine underwent further development by Aurelio Lampredi. This consisted of an increase in displacement to 2,341 cm³, obtained by an increase in bore. Thus the 195 series was born, the Inter version of which appeared in the second half of the year. The basic models having only one carburetor, produced 135 hp at 6,000 rpm. The greatest Italian stylists of the time were also engaged in building the bodywork of the 195 Inter — which had almost entirely the same mechanics of the earlier 166

— although none of them ever built a cabriolet version. Production, which lasted the space of a single year, resulted in 19 cars, with bodies by Vignale, Ghia and Touring. In addition, there were three coupés built by the Swiss Ghia SA company of Aigle, based upon Michelotti's designs.

In 1951, in wake of a line of development that constantly increased the displacement, the 212 Inter appeared. The engine now had an engine capacity of 2,562 cm³ and generated 150 hp at 6,500 rpm, as compared to the 170 hp of the short wheelbase Export version meant for racing (chassis with even numbers). Once again, it was the one or three carburetor feed which determined a greater or lesser horsepower, the choice being left to the client. However, Export models clearly intended for use on the road were not lacking, just as several Inter cars did not disdain from taking part in races on various occasions. Depending on the axle ratio chosen, the single carburetor version could reach a maximum speed of 113 mph (183 km/h) or 121 mph (196 km/h).

In all, twenty two 212 Exports were produced, primarily in the Touring "barchetta" version and the Vignale coupé version. On the other hand, 84 Inters were produced, including a good number of coupés by Vignale, which also built several spider and cabriolet versions. A large quantity of the coupé and cabriolet versions were also built by Pininfarina. The production of 212 Inters represented the beginning of an extremely close working relationship with Ferrari.

Open, coupé and also 2 + 2 versions were among those built by Ghia, while Touring prepared one car with "barchetta" bodywork, as well as a few coupés. A cabriolet was also built by Abbott, while a coupé was fitted with bodywork in the Stabilimenti Farina.

Lastly, it should be mentioned that in the second and final year of its life, 1952, the 212 Inter underwent several mechanical improvements which mainly concerned the steering unit.

Technical data

MODEL 212 INTER
YEAR OF PRODUCTION 1951-1952

ENGINE
position: front longitudinal; **cylinders:** 60° 12V-cm³ 2, 562; **compression:** 8,0:1; **feed:** 1 Weber 36DCF carburetor; **ignition:** single; **timing:** 2 valves per cylinder-1 OHC per bank chain driven; **max power:** 110 kW (150 hp) at 6,500 rpm.

CHASSIS
gearbox: 4-speed + reverse; **suspensions:** front: wishbones/coil springs — rear: rigid axle/longitudinal leaf springs; **brakes:** front: drums —rear: drums; **wheelbase** (mm): 2,600.

This 195 Inter by Vignale from a Michelotti design dates to 1951.

The 212 Inter with 2 + 2 coupé bodywork by Pininfarina.

340-342-375 AMERICA / 250 EUROPA

The command of Ferrari's technical management by Aurelio Lampredi can be linked to the decision to concentrate on high engine capacities, over 3 liters, in order to meet the demands of the North American market. Although lacking any revolutionary changes with regard to Gioachino Colombo's engine, the new "long" 12 thus came into being, with a greater wheelbase between the cylinders to allow for a considerable increase in bore. Created as a 3.3-liter, at the beginning of 1950, within the space of just one year this engine was subject to two further increases displacement in the racing versions, first to 4.1 liters and then to 4.5. Conceived primarily for racing, the engine had several new features including cylinder liners screwed to the heads in order to guarantee maximum holding. This completely eliminated the traditional seal. The new engine appeared for the first time on a Grand Tourer at the Paris Show in October, 1950, under the bonnet of the new 340 America. It was a 4,102 cm³ version fed by three carburetors and with a reduced power of 220 hp at 6,000 rpm.

This car had a ladder frame chassis that was not unlike that of the earlier Ferraris, as was also true of the suspensions, with transverse leaf springs to the front and longitudinal leaf springs to the rear integrated by hydraulic lever dampers. It had a five speed gearbox.

In this new series of automobiles the emphasis was still placed on the racing nature of the car, so much so that eight, of the 25 produced, adopted an engine with dry sump lubrication. In addition, only very few were built in an obviously "touring" design. The latter group included a 2 + 2 with bodywork by Ghia and a coupé by Vignale. At the end of 1952, the road versions of the 340 made way for the new 342 America, with which Ferrari, for the first time, aimed to meet the demands of a certain clientele that would never have found itself driving on the race track. Left-handed drive was adopted, as well as a 4-speed synchronized gearbox. However, the power only slightly increased to 230 hp at the same number of rpm. The chassis had a longer wheelbase,

The two-seater 250 Europa coupé designed by Pininfarina in 1953.

although it retained the traditional "ladder" structure of the previous model. Production of the 342 was very limited, as far as both time (from October 1952 until the following January) and numbers were concerned (six being built in all). Five were fitted with bodywork by Pininfarina in coupé and cabriolet versions, in addition to a single coupé by Vignale. They were particularly carefully built cars, meant for clients who were just as particular, including King Leopold of Belgium, who acquired the first Pininfarina cabriolet.

In 1953, the new 375 America was presented with a 4,523 cm³ engine and three carburetors, generating 300 hp at 6,300 rpm. Depending on which of the four axle ratios available adopted, the maximum speed ranged from 144 mph (232 km/h) to 155 mph (250 km/h). As for the chassis, the 375 utilized a new structure copied from that of the 1952 250 MM and consisting of four large elliptic longitudinal side members, two external ones and two in-

In 1953, Pininfarina also provided the 250 Europa with this 2 + 2 coupé bodywork.

Ferrari 375 America

ternal ones (integrated with thin tubular struts) which met up at the level of the rear axle. The wheelbase was further lengthened to 9 feet 2 inches (2,800 mm), the largest ever used by a Ferrari. The suspensions retained the pattern of the 340 and 342. One car was later fitted with coil springs, instead of leaf springs.

In 1953 at the Paris Show, the 250 Europa made its debut at the same time as the 375 America. They were almost identical, except for the former's smaller engine capacity. On this occasion, Lampredi's ''long'' engine, reduced to 2,963 cm³ and with a 240 hp at 7,000 rpm, was also chosen for this 3-liter car. The bodywork was built for both cars by Pininfarina and, to a lesser extent, by Vignale and Ghia. In this case too, there were no apparent differences between the two cars. Very limited production resulted in 13 375 Americas and 17 250 Europas.

Technical data

MODEL 375 AMERICA
YEAR OF PRODUCTION 1953-1955

ENGINE
position: front longitudinal; **cylinders:** 60° 12V-cm³ 4,523; **compression:** 8,0:1; **feed:** 3 Weber 40DCF carburetors; **ignition:** single; **timing:** 2 valves per cylinder - 1 OHC per bank chain driven; **max power:** 221 kW (300 hp) at 6,300 rpm.

CHASSIS
gearbox: 4-speed + reverse; **suspensions:** front: wishbones/coil springs — rear: rigid axle/longitudinal leaf springs; **brakes:** front: drums — rear: drums; **wheelbase** (mm): 2,800.

This Pininfarina 375 America cabriolet appeared in 1955.

This original coupé by Pininfarina was the last of the 375 Americas (1955).

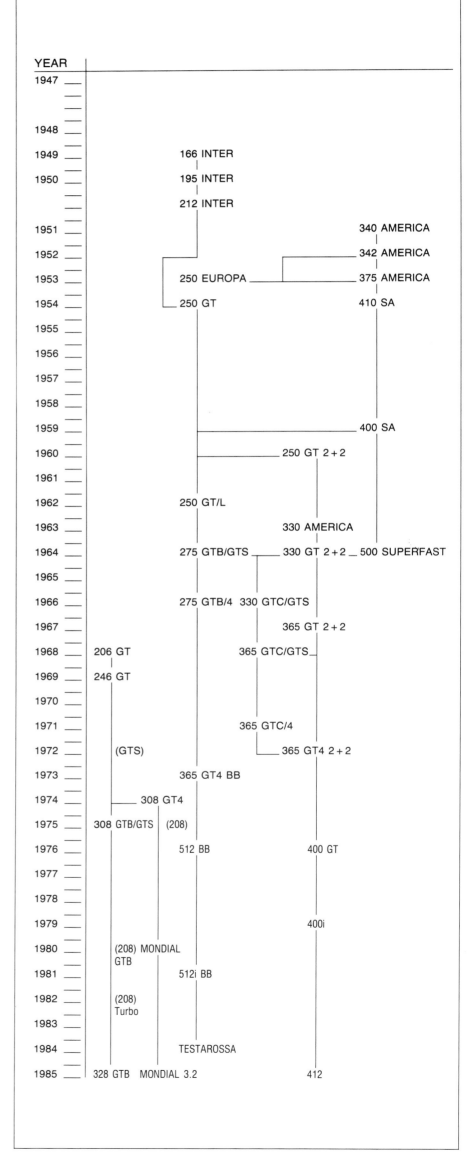

GRAND TOURERS

YEAR

1947
1948
1949 — 166 INTER
1950 — 195 INTER
212 INTER
1951 — 340 AMERICA
1952 — 342 AMERICA
1953 — 250 EUROPA — 375 AMERICA
1954 — 250 GT — 410 SA
1955
1956
1957
1958
1959 — 400 SA
1960 — 250 GT 2 + 2
1961
1962 — 250 GT/L
1963 — 330 AMERICA
1964 — 275 GTB/GTS — 330 GT 2 + 2 — 500 SUPERFAST
1965
1966 — 275 GTB/4 330 GTC/GTS
1967 — 365 GT 2 + 2
1968 — 206 GT — 365 GTC/GTS
1969 — 246 GT
1970
1971 — 365 GTC/4
1972 — (GTS) — 365 GT4 2 + 2
1973 — 365 GT4 BB
1974 — 308 GT4
1975 — 308 GTB/GTS (208)
1976 — 512 BB — 400 GT
1977
1978
1979 — 400i
1980 — (208) MONDIAL GTB
1981 — 512i BB
1982 — (208) Turbo
1983
1984 — TESTAROSSA
1985 — 328 GTB MONDIAL 3.2 — 412

410-400 SUPERAMERICA / 500 SUPERFAST

The dynasty of Superamericas had its ancestry in the 410 of 1955, which took the place of the 375 America, substantially repeating its technical characteristics. In addition, it began improvements similar to those of the 250 GT. In fact, the chassis was new, with side members that passed over the rear axle at the back. Two wheelbase variants were adopted, one identical to the 375 and the other shortened by about eight inches (20 cm). The tracks were also widened. The front suspensions definitively adopted coil springs, instead of transverse leaf springs. In the rear the lever dampers were placed in a new position beneath the above mentioned side members. The engine, which still belonged to the Lampredi series, was increased to 4,963 cm³, obtaining 340 hp at 6,000 rpm. There was a single camshaft for every row of cylinders, while the feed repeated the earlier choice of three twin barrel carburetors. Unlike the earlier versions, the spark plugs were situated inside of the cylinder banks. The gearbox remained a 4-speed synchronized one. The maximum speed with the differ ent available axle ratios ranged from 136 mph (220 km/h) to 161 mph (260 km/h).

The first model of the 410 was presented at the Brussels Show in 1956, with lines designed by Pininfarina. The Grugliasco-based body-maker was subsequently commissioned to build 13 of the 16 first series 410 Superamericas which were produced until the following year. The very original coupé, with bodywork by Ghia, and two cars, a coupé and a cabriolet, were built by Boano. Apart from these, mention should be made of a single car, designated Superfast, which was presented in Paris in 1956. On a short wheelbase chassis, this model united the Pininfarina coupé bodywork (characterized by large rear fins) and the 410 Sport's engine (with dual ignition, and capable of 380 hp at 7,000 rpm).

From 1956 onwards, the 410 was offered in a production series version with a short wheelbase of 8 feet 6 inches (2,600 mm). This gave rise to what could officially be defined the second series. Eight of these cars were produced, one with bodywork by Scaglietti and seven with bodywork by Pininfarina. The latter included the second of the single 4.9 Superfast presented at the 1957 Turin Show and fitted, unlike the first, with a single ignition engine. In this model, the bicolored bodywork, that now lacked the showy fins, reached a rare aesthetic balance between the purity of the Italian lines and American taste.

In 1958, the Superamerica underwent a series of modifications, including the spark plugs' transposition to the cylinder banks' exterior. This solution resulted in a better restructured combustion chamber and a consequent increase in power to 360 hp at 7,000 rpm. The short wheelbase chassis was adapted (for this higher performance) by an increase in the brake drums' diameter, while the standard bodywork for the 12 cars produced up till the end of 1959 was equal to that to the 4.9 Superfast.

Although it retained the designation Superamerica, the new 400 SA — which appeared at the Turin Show in 1959 with the Pininfarina Coupé Speciale built for Gianni Agnelli and presented in its definitive form at the Bruxelles Show in January, 1960 — originated from an entirely new project. The chassis was similar to the GT 250's layout, with a wheelbase of 8 feet (2,440 mm). The suspension systems remained the same; however, the 400 SAs were provided with telescopic dampers instead of lever ones. The car was also fitted with four disc brakes. The engine, measuring 3,967 cm³, was no longer derived from Lampredi's "long" 12-V, but from Colombo's "short" 12-V. As a result, it had considerably increased bore and stroke. It had single camshaft timing with a coil spring valve recall, while the feed was guaranteed by three twin barrel carburetors, releasing 340 hp at 7,000 rpm. There was a 4-speed gearbox with electric overdrive in fourth gear.

The bodywork followed two parallel lines of development. One

The 400 SA cabriolet by Pininfarina presented at the 1962 Geneva Show.

In 1964, the 500 Superfast replaced the Superamerica series.

was the more classic Pininfarina cabriolet and the other a Coupé Aerodinamica based on the only Superfast II which the same body-maker had presented at the Turin Show in 1960. Up till 1962, five cabriolets and 12 coupés were built. That year, at the Geneva Show, a new single car was presented, the Superfast III, with its typical retractable front headlamps. It was followed almost immediately by the Superfast IV with dual headlamps. This was merely a Superfast II with new bodywork. In 1962, the Superamerica's wheelbase was also increased to 8 feet 6 inches (2,600 mm), giving rise to the second series, which remained in production for another two years without any significant mechanical changes. In this series, four cabriolets and 19 aerodynamic coupés were produced. In March 1964, the last car traceable to this line of descent, the 500 Superfast, came into being. Its unusual engine was a single camshaft long 12-V fitted with the removable heads of the Colombo engine. The displacement was 4,962 cm³ and, with three carburetor feed, its power reached 400 hp at 6,500 rpm.

This car, which was truly unique in terms of comfort, finish, and power, was built in two series. The first, of which 24 were built, adopted a chassis similar to that of the 330 GT 2 + 2. The second, (12 vehicles produced) which appeared in 1966, had the same modifications carried out on the 1965 car, including the adoption of a 5-speed synchronized gearbox.

Technical data

MODEL 400 SUPERAMERICA (SUPERFAST IV)
YEAR OF PRODUCTION 1962

ENGINE
position: front longitudinal; **cylinders:** 60° 12V-cm³ 3,967; **compression:** 8,8:1; **feed:** 3 Weber 46DCF carburetors; **ignition:** single; **timing:** 2 valves per cylinder-1 OHC per bank chain driven; **max power:** 250 kW (340 hp) at 7,000 rpm.

CHASSIS
gearbox: 4-speed + reverse; **suspensions:** front: wishbones/coil springs — rear: rigid axle/longitudinal leaf springs; **brakes:** front: discs — rear: discs; **wheelbase** (mm): 2,420.

Ferrari 400 Superamerica (Superfast IV)

Ferrari 275 GTB

275 GTB-GTS-GTB/4

The 275 GTB was an important project for Ferrari, created in order to give the 250 GT roadster a worthy descendant. Presented at the Paris Show in October, 1964, this "berlinetta" was the first Maranello-built car to adopt modifications such as four wheel independent suspension, "transaxle" transmission with gearbox in unit with the rear differential, and a specially studied 5-speed gearbox. The chassis was still a ladder frame with complex tubular structures supporting the engine, the transaxle unit, and the suspensions. As far as the latter were concerned, both front and rear axles adopted a system of twin wishbones with Koni dampers and coil spring struts. The bodywork, which had a notable reinforcing function, was presented in two versions, both designed by Pininfarina, the GTB coupé produced by Scaglietti and the GTS spider built by the same Turin-based body builder. The engine constituted the final evolution of the 12-V originally designed by Colombo, and was reamed still further to obtain a displacement of 3,286 cm³. The timing operated by a single camshaft per cylinder bank driven by a triple chain. The valves were activated by roller followers and rocker arms. In the basic version, with three twin barrel carburetors, the power reached 260 hp at 7,400 rpm, although for clients who wanted a still higher performance a version with six twin barrel carburetors was available, producing 280 hp at 7,600 rpm. Early in 1965, some modifications to the car's appearance were carried out, including an enlarged rear window, although a true second series was presented a year later. The main aim of this was to correct some of the defects of the former. The nose, which in the earlier structure had caused an excessive front lift at high speeds, was redesigned in a slightly longer version which also improved the car's penetration coefficient.

Moreover, the driveshaft which linked the engine with the transaxle unit and had previously been subject to excessive vibrations, was enclosed in a torque tube which rigidly joined the engine to the transmission. This also improved chassis' resistance to bending. Furthermore, this modification meant that the engine could be mounted on elastic supports with the aim of reducing vibrations and noise inside the cockpit. Lastly, the lubrication system adopted the dry sump type.

Several cars designated 275 GTB/C were produced for racing, based on the second series 275 with an aluminum bodywork. This model's racing career was rather limited because it was not built expressly for this purpose. However, results were not lacking, as an outright third place was obtained by Mairesse and Beurlys at Le Mans.

An important development marked the new version of this car presented at the Paris Show in 1966 and designated 275 GTB/4. For the first time a production Ferrari adopted a system of double overhead camshafts, following a pattern that had been introduced on Colombo's 12-V in the Sports-Prototypes of 1957. As far as appearance was concerned, the new solution was apparent in the central projection that ran along the entire length of the bonnet, made necessary due to the system's greater vertical dimensions. The new twin camshaft, fed by six carburetors, did not have a greater power, which remained at 280 hp at 7,700 rpm, although it allowed for the engine to be better exploited.

At the initiative of the American importer Luigi Chinetti, Scaglietti built a very limited series of cars in a GTS/4 spider version directly derived from the coupé.

The 275 went out of production in 1968, after about 950 had been produced. Of these (and these figures should be considered merely approximate), 250 and 200 were first and second series GTBs, respectively, 200 were GTSs, 10 were GTB/Cs, 280 were GTB/4s, and 9 were GTS/4s.

Technical data

MODEL 275 GTB	
YEAR OF PRODUCTION 1964-1966	

ENGINE
position: front longitudinal; **cylinders:** 60° 12V-cm³ 3,286; **compression:** 9,2:1; **feed:** 3 Weber 40DCZ6 carburetors; **ignition:** single; **timing:** 2 valves per cylinder-1 OHC per bank chain driven; **max power:** 191 kW (280 hp) at 7,600 rpm.

CHASSIS
gearbox: 5-speed + reverse; **suspensions:** front: wishbones/coil springs — rear: wishbones/coil springs; **brakes:** front: discs — rear: discs; **wheelbase** (mm): 2,400.

The GTS version of the 275 was provided with spider bodywork built by Pininfarina.

250 GT

From 1954 to 1964, approximately 2,500 250 GTs were built. This was a dynasty of Grand Tourers which was based on the 250 Europa, differing from it due to a series of fundamental innovations. Apart from an entirely new chassis, it was with this car that Ferrari returned to the generation of 60° V-12 engines whose roots lay in Gioachino Colombo's initial project. It was a 2,593 cm³ over squared engine which had been used on the 250 MM in 1952. This engine, made entirely of light alloy, was characterized by a single camshaft with slanted valves controlled by roller-mounted rocker arms. The power of the road versions was initially 200 hp at 6,600 rpm. This gradually increased until it reached 250 hp at 7,400 rpm in 1960. The racing versions eventually generated about 280 hp. In the course of its ten year career, the 250 GT was subject to numerous and frequent modifications. One of the most important of these was the replacement of the drum brake by the disc brake which occurred in 1959. The front wheel suspension consisted of wishbones and coil springs. In the rear, an unsprung axle with semi-elliptic leaf springs, two trailing radius arms, and hydraulic dampers was utilized.

The chassis consisted of a tubular space frame with a wheelbase of 8 ft 6 in (2,600 mm), which in 1959 was joined by a short wheelbase variant measuring 7 ft 10 in (2,400 mm). An unofficial classification was used to distinguish these two versions, which were known as LWB and SWB (standing for Long and Short wheelbase, respectively).

The first 250 GT appeared at the Paris Show in 1954, with a Pininfarina coupé body, which was subsequently followed by numerous versions designed by the most famous Italian body builders. The best known of the series is probably the short wheelbase Berlinetta of 1959, the car that perhaps more than any other succeeded in embodying the Ferrari concept of cars for dual use: both on the road and the race track.

The body was built with a Pininfarina design by Scaglietti. In the standard versions it was steel and aluminum (doors and bonnet), while in the versions intended for racing, in which the 250 GT scored outstanding results, it was entirely aluminum. Since it lacked GT rating, it was forced to compete initially in the Sports category. Subsequently it obtained this rating in 1960, and the

The 2+2 250 GT was presented at the Paris Show in 1960.

Berlinetta won the Tourist Trophy in 1960 and 1961 with Stirling Moss at the wheel. It also won the Tour de France three years running (1959-1961). Another important result was first place in the GT category in the Le Mans 24-Hour race in 1961, as well as an outright victory in the Monthléry 1,000-km race of the same year.

The 250 GT is also remembered from its famous spider versions. The first prototype appeared at the Geneva Show in 1956, with bodywork by Boano, to whom Pininfarina entrusted other projects the following year. These included a spider for Peter Collins, who had disc brakes mounted on it in England, thus appearing for the first time on a Maranello-built car. In 1957, series production began with the 250 GT Cabriolet designed and built by Pininfarina, followed at the end of the year by the Spider California, once again designed by the Turin stylist, but built by Scaglietti. Two series of the convertible were produced, 36 of the first and 200 of the second. 47 of the first version of the California with long wheelbase were built until 1960 by Maranello as well as 57 of the second short wheelbase series, which were available until 1960. Intended mainly for the United States, the open versions of the 250 GT had a sporting career worthy of respect, both in America and Europe, thanks to the California versions which obtained the best results in the 1959 season, with a victory in the GT class in the Sebring 12-Hour race and fifth place in the Le Mans 24-Hour. The 250 GT long wheelbase chassis was the first in which Ferrari put a 2+2 version into production. Designed by Pininfarina, this car was presented in 1960, after the basic characteristics had been developed by means of two experimental prototypes. The engine was moved forward to create a large space, while the search for greater comfort led to the installation of a 4-speed synchromesh with automatic overdrive in fourth gear.

The short wheelbase 250 GT "berlinetta" was produced from 1959 until 1962.

The Pininfarina coupé version of the 250 GT of 1958.

Technical data

MODEL 250 GT SPIDER CALIFORNIA
YEAR OF PRODUCTION 1958-1963

ENGINE
position: front longitudinal; **cylinders:** 60° 12V-cm³ 2,953; **compression:** 9,5:1; **feed:** 3 Weber 40DCL6 or 42DCL3 carburetors; **ignition:** single; **timing:** 2 valves per cylinder-1 OHC per bank chain driven; **max power:** 206 kW (280 hp) at 7,000 rpm.

CHASSIS
gearbox: 4-speed + reverse; **suspensions:** front: wishbones/coil springs — rear: rigid axle/longitudinal leaf springs; **brakes:** front: discs — rear: discs (from 1959); **wheelbase** (mm): 2,400.

Ferrari 250 GT Spider California

Ferrari 365 GT 2+2

330 GT 2+2 / 365 GT 2+2-GTC4-GT4 2+2 400 - 412

Ferrari's habit of accompanying its more sporty models with less showy four-seater versions which had begun with the 1960 250 GT, continued with the 330 GT 2+2 presented at the Brussels Show in 1964. An engine derived from the 12-V Superamerica was chosen for this car, with an engine capacity of 3,967 cm³ and a power of 290 hp at 7,000 rpm. The timing was single camshaft and the feed consisted of three twin barrel carburetors. A 4-speed gearbox with overdrive on the fourth gear was situated in unit with the engine. The chassis was the classic square section tubular space frame, and there were no substantial modifications compared to the previous model, even as far as the suspensions were concerned.

These retained the rigid rear axle with longitudinal leaf springs, while in the front there were wishbones with coil springs. The brakes were of the disc type with servo. In 1965, after the car had been on the market for a year, numerous modifications were carried out. As far as the bodywork was concerned, the double headlamps which Pininfarina had used to characterize the nose were replaced by single ones, which were, above all, more in accordance with European taste. The Borrani wire wheels were replaced by alloy rims. From a mechanical point of view, the most significant innovation was the adoption of a completely synchronized gearbox.

After almost 1,000 330s had been produced, the car made way for the 365 GT 2+2 in 1967. The latter made its debut at the Paris Show. With this model, which was more than 15 feet (5 m) long, Ferrari aimed for the first time to meet the needs of a certain clientele that not only desired exceptional performance, but also a superior level of comfort. With this in mind, rear independent suspension was adopted with a hydropneumatic self-levelling system as well as servo steering.

The level of the finish in the cockpit was also carefully studied, with noise and vibrations being reduced to a minimum. The car's lines, again designed by Pininfarina, were influenced, as far as the nose was concerned, by the 500 Superfast, and generally repeated the stylistic layout of the 330 GT Speciale (which had been presented a year earlier). The engine, with a capacity of 4,390 cm³, retained the single camshaft timing and three carburetor feed and was capable of generating 320 hp at 6,600 rpm. Approximately 200 of these cars were built before production ceased in 1971. In the same year the new 365 GTC4 appeared. This model could not be described as the conceptual heir of the earlier 2+2, due to its more sporty lines, its shorter wheelbase, and the cramped nature of the two rear seats. At the same time as far as the engine was concerned it constituted the prefiguration of the next four-seater that was to appear in 1972. Although the engine retained the same capacity, it was provided with twin camshafts and fed by six twin barrel carburetors, no longer placed between the 2-cylinder banks, but to the exterior of the V which they formed. The aim behind this modification was to reduce harmful emissions from the exhaust. The power remained the same, but it was now obtained at 7,700 rpm. In this form, the 12-V was used on the new 365 GT4 2+2. The latter had completely new and advanced bodywork, designed as usual by Pininfarina and mounted on a chassis that was once again a tubular space frame, although the wheelbase was lengthened to 8 feet 10 inches (2,700 mm) compared to the 8 feet 8 inches (2,650 mm) of the previous 250, 330, and 365 models. In October 1976, the new 400 version was introduced into the market in two variants, the Automatica and the GT. The former adopted — for the first time in the history of the Maranello company — a 3-speed automatic gearbox produced by General Motors. The displacement was increased to 4,823 cm³, generating a power of 340 hp at 6,500 rpm.

The bodywork differed from that of the 365 possessing a lower spoiler and supplementary headlamps below the bumpers in the front (as well as the addition of rear lights). In 1979, a K-Jetronic mechanical injection system was adopted for the renewed 400i, with a new modification of the engine in conjunction with the antipollution laws in the United States. The result was a reduction in power to 310 hp (later increased to 315) at 6,400 rpm. The 400/400i series was built from 1976 to 1984, and of the 1,810 cars completed, 1,239 were automatic.

A further increase in the engine capacity to 4,943 cm³ was introduced in the 412, which went into production in 1985 with slight modifications in appearance and a power of 340 hp at 6,000 rpm. With this model, brakes with a ABS anti-skid device were adopted on a Ferrari car.

Technical data

MODEL 365 GT 2+2
YEAR OF PRODUCTION 1967-1971

ENGINE
position: front longitudinal; **cylinders:** 60° 12V-cm³ 4,390; **compression:** 8,8:1; **feed:** 3 Weber 40DF1/5 carburetors; **ignition:** single; **timing:** 2 valves per cylinder-1 OHC per bank chain driven; **max power:** 235 kW (320 hp) at 6,600 rpm.

CHASSIS
gearbox: 5-speed + reverse; **suspensions:** front: wishbones/coil springs — rear: wishbones/coil springs/hydropneumatic level regulator; **brakes:** front: discs — rear: discs; **wheelbase** (mm): 2,650.

The 2+2 330 GT was created in January 1964, with four headlamps to the front.

Production of the 365 GTC4 was limited to 1971-72.

365 GTB/4 DAYTONA

Until 1971 for the European market original headlamps protected by a perspex fascia were adopted on the Daytona.

The cars meant for export to the United States had retractable type front headlamps instead.

While other manufacturers had already opted for a rear central engine, like Lamborghini, Ferrari remained faithful to the 275 GTB's traditional pattern, also in the subsequent 365 GTB/4. This was introduced at the Paris Show in 1968, and is better known as the Daytona. With this car, the Maranello company definitively abandoned the 12-V engine of the Colombo series. It took up once more, also in its own more sporty model, the engine originally designed by Lampredi which equipped the more sedate Grand Tourers of the 330/365 GT series. Compared to these, the most obvious modification introduced to the Daytona was the adoption of twin camshaft timing. The displacement was 4,390 cm³, and appeared for the first time in 1964 in this series of engines with the single camshaft 365 P. It generated 352 hp at 7,500 rpm, allowing the car to reach 180 mph (290 km/h). Moreover, this outstanding maximum speed was favored by the remarkable aerodynamics of the body which, in this case too, was built by Scaglietti with a design modified for Pininfarina by Leonardo Fioravanti.

The engine feed made use of six twin barrel carburetors, while the lubrication was of the dry sump type. The mechanical structure once again repeated the transaxle pattern, with a more rigid tubular space frame than that of the 275. Compared to the latter, wider tracks were adopted, and the brake system was improved by ventilated discs with a greater diameter, made possible by the use of 15'' rims instead of 14''. The suspensions were once again double wishbones with coil springs. The car as a whole was rather heavy, but the power and elasticity of the engine, as well as the stability derived from the correct distribution of the masses on two axles, not only made the Daytona an extremely fast car, but also a one that was very stable and safe. Unlike the previous Ferrari berlinettas, the Daytona did not undergo substantial modifications over the years. Only the nose appearance, which originally had a perspex fascia running along its entire width that also served as housing for the headlamps, was modified. In the version meant for the United States, this fascia was made of aluminum with retractable headlamps. In 1971, these two variants were united with the adoption of retractable headlamps and a fascia in the same color as the bodywork. The Daytona scored some notable successes in races. Rated in the GT special category or Group 4 on January 1, 1972, the 365 GTB/4 was adopted on the race track above all by Georges Filipinetti's Belgian team, Luigi Chinetti's NART and a team managed by the French importer of the car. Some of the most important results included fifth place in the 1972 Le Mans 24-Hour with Andruet and Ballot-Lena at the wheel, and the victory in the 1973 Tour de France with a crew consisting of Andruet and Biche. Numerous cars of this types, built expressly for racing, used large quantities of aluminum and synthetic materials.

It is strange to note how, for its own high performance Grand Tourer, Ferrari did not at the time adopt a central engine which had already been introduced successfully in the 250 Le Mans in 1964. However, even in its traditional structure, the Daytona remained the world's fastest production series car for a long time. The earlier engine received a worthy swan song at Maranello, and with the introduction of the new 365 BB in 1973, was used solely in the 2 + 2 400 and 412 series.

Approximately 1,500 Daytonas were built. Of these just over 100 in the spider version that was presented at the Frankfurt Show in 1969 were made.

Technical data

MODEL 365 GTB/4 DAYTONA YEAR OF PRODUCTION 1969-1973
ENGINE **position:** front longitudinal; **cylinders:** 60° 12V-cm³ 4,390; **compression:** 8,8:1; **feed:** 6 Weber 40DCN carburetors; **ignition:** single; **timing:** 2 valves per cylinder-2 OHC per bank chain driven; **max power:** 259 kW (352 hp) at 7,500 rpm.
CHASSIS **gearbox:** 5-speed + reverse; **suspensions:** front: wishbones/coil springs — rear: wishbones/coil springs; **brakes:** front: discs — rear: discs; **wheelbase** (mm): 2,400.

The spider version of the Daytona presented at Frankfurt in 1969.

Ferrari 365 GTB/4 Daytona

Ferrari 328 GTS

246 GT-GTS / 308 GTB-GTS-GTB-4 328 GTB-GTS / Mondial

In 1968, under the name of Dino, a series of cars with rear central engine mounted in a transverse position was introduced. A 65° 6-V engine that had been designed for races by Vittorio Jano was adopted, having been subsequently adapted for series production by Franco Rocchi. With an engine capacity of 1,987 cm³ and fed by three twin barrel carburetors, the 206 GT had a power of 180 hp at 8,000 rpm. The timing was gear-driven twin camshaft, and the car also had Magneti Marelli electronic ignition. The 5-speed gearbox and the final transmission were mounted below the engine.

The bodywork, designed by Pininfarina, marked the completion of perfecting the car which had begun in 1965, when a first prototype with longitudinal engine was presented at the Paris Show. In 1969, following a limited series of approximately 150 cars, the 246 GT was created, with an increased engine capacity of 2,416 cm³. The single-block, no longer in light alloy but in cast iron, was now produced by Fiat, which used it on its own sports cars, which were also christened Dino. The power increased to 195 hp at 7,600 rpm, although this increase did not noticeably improve the performance, due to the overall weight increase that characterized the new version.

The bodywork which, for example, had been entirely aluminum in the case of the 206, was now executed in steel. It proved to be more comfortable, thanks also to a slight increase in the wheelbase of 22 inches (58 cm). The only stylistic differences in the 246 GT were the wheels with traditional attachments instead of the rapid assembly wing nut, and the fuel cap which was protected by a small flap. Up till 1974, 2,700 246s were built in the GT version, as well as 1,200 in the open GTS version that was introduced in 1972.

The 308 GTB was called upon in 1975 to replace the first generation of Dino Ferraris, together with the less successful 308 GT4 2 + 2 (with bodywork by Bertone) that had been created a year earlier. The new car abandoned the Dino trademark to assume, not only de facto, but also formally, the rank of an authentic Ferrari. The 90° 8-cylinder V engine, entirely in light alloy, was capable of generating 255 hp at 770 rpm. Its most outstanding characteristics were twin camshaft timing with cogged belt, feed with four twin barrel carburetors, and dry sump lubrication. The chassis, as usual, was a tubular space frame, with bodywork in fiberglass. It was replaced by one in steel in 1977, at the time that the open GTS version went on the market.

In the case of both the GT4 and the GTB a version with a reduced engine capacity of 1,990 cm³ was built, exclusively for the Italian market: the 208 GT4 of 1975 with a power of 180 hp at 7,700 rpm and the 208 GTB created in 1980 with an 8-V generating 155 hp at 6,800 rpm.

Two years after its presentation, the latter was replaced by the 208 Turbo, fitted with a KKK turbocharger with maximum pressure of 0.6 bar and Bosch K-Jetronic injection, capable of developing 220 hp at 7,000 rpm. From 1981 onwards, the same type of mechanical injection had also been installed on the 3-liter versions. However, the result had not been an increase in power. It actually diminished to 214 hp at 6,600 rpm, but there was a reduction in harmful emissions. In 1982, the 308 GTBi and GTSi made up for the lost hp with the Quattrovalvole versions, capable of generating 240 hp at 7,700 rpm (in which the dry sump lubrication system was abandoned).

In 1980, all the versions of the GT4 had made way·for the new Mondial 8. With this car the 214 hp injection engine had made its debut, before it, too, adopted the 32-valve version.

In 1985, all the 8-cylinder Ferraris benefited from an increase in engine capacity to 3,185 cm³, obtaining 270 hp at 7,000 rpm. The new 328 GTB/GTS and Mondial 3.2 versions also received several modifications to their noses and the tails.

The 208 Turbo was also subjected to development in 1985, with an increase in power to 254 hp at 6,500 rpm. This was made possible by the adoption of a heat exchanger and a new IHI water-cooled turbocompressor, capable of providing a supercharged pressure of 1.05 bar.

Technical data

MODEL 328 GTS
YEAR OF PRODUCTION 1985

ENGINE
position: rear central transverse; **cylinders:** 90° 8V-cm³ 3,185; **compression:** 9,8:1; **feed:** K-Jetronic mechanical injection; **ignition:** single; **timing:** 4 valves per cylinder-2 OHC per bank chain belt driven; **max power:** 199 kW (270 hp) at 7,000 rpm.

CHASSIS
gearbox: 5-speed + reverse; **suspensions:** front: wishbones/coil springs — rear: wishbones/coil springs; **brakes:** front: ventilated discs — rear: ventilated discs; **wheelbase** (mm): 2,350.

The Dino 246 GT was introduced at the end of 1969, while the open GTS version was created three years later.

BB / TESTAROSSA

The Pininfarina-designed P6 of 1968 established the stylistic basis for the 12-cylinder berlinettas with rear engine.

In the early 1970s, Ferrari wished to repeat the layout of the boxer engine which had been successfully introduced in the single-seater Formula One cars during the 1970 season, in series production. Thus, the following year, the 365 BB (Berlinetta Boxer) was presented at the Turin Show. It was a two-seater coupé provided with an entirely new 12 opposed cylinders engine mounted in a rear longitudinal position. It had dry sump lubrication and a differential-gearbox unit that was uniquely situated below the engine. The power was transmitted from the flywheel to the gearbox by means of three drop gears. This solution was adopted in order to reduce the length of the engine and provide more comfort. However, this modification impeded the baricenter from being low enough to obtain a suitable trim for racing track use. The crankshaft was fitted with seven bearings. The heads and cylinders were identical to those of the earlier Daytona, with the same engine capacity of 4,390 cm³, but with an increase in power to 360 hp at 7,500 rpm.

The feed was entrusted to four Weber triple barrel carburetors, while the timing system consisted of two valves per cylinder controlled by two overhead camshafts for every bank of cylinders worked by means of a cogged belt.

The chassis consisted of a steel tubular space frame with the engine and transmission being supported by an auxiliary sub-frame. The four wheel independent suspension adopted a wishbone system for both axles with double dampers in the rear.

In 1976, the engine capacity was increased to 4,942 cm³ in the new 512 BB version, conceived above all with the aim of reducing harmful emissions from the exhaust. However, a notable increase in the maximum torque was accompanied by a reduction in power to 340 hp at 6,500 rpm. The final version of the Berlinetta Boxer was the 512i of 1981, fitted with a K-Jetronic injection system for an unvaried power although obtained at 6,000 rpm. The maximum speed of this version was 174 mph (280 km/h), with an acceleration from 0 to 62 mph (0 to 100 km/h) in 6,2 seconds.

The lines of the Berlinetta Boxer were designed by Pininfarina according to the aesthetic dictates of the P6 prototype realized in 1968. The chassis was designed by Angelo Bellei, while the engine development was the work of Giuliano De Angelis.

In 1984, after more than 2,500 had been produced, this car made way for the Testarossa, which was based mechanically on an identical layout as far as both the chassis and engine were concerned. Notable innovations were the adoption of lateral coolers and timing of four valves per cylinder, which allowed for an increase to 390 hp at 6,300 rpm.

As far as the chassis was concerned, there was a remarkable increase in the rear track which notably reduced the tendency to roll caused by the "raised" position of the engine.

The bodywork was entirely new, once again designed by Pininfarina and characterized primarily by large lateral air inlets for the coolers.

The remarkable emphasis placed on aerodynamic research led to a penetration co-efficient (Cx) of 0.36, with notably reduced lift co-efficients of 0.01 and 0.017 for the front and rear axles, respectively.

BB and Testarossa both represent the maximum expression of the high performance sports car, although both are rather unsuited to be successfully used in racing (unlike the earlier 275 GTB and Daytona) due to the car chassis which, following the changing demands of the clientele, reflected the need to offer, even in the case of thoroughbreds such as these, a cockpit that was sufficiently spacious and comfortable.

Technical data

MODEL TESTAROSSA
YEAR OF PRODUCTION 1984

ENGINE
position: rear central longitudinal; **cylinders:** 180° 12V-cm³ 4,942; **compression:** 9,3:1; **feed:** K-Jetronic mechanical injection; **ignition:** single; **timing:** 4 valves per cylinder-2 OHC per bank chain belt driven; **max power:** 287 kW (390 hp) at 6,300 rpm.

CHASSIS
gearbox: 5-speed + reverse; **suspensions:** front: wishbones/coil springs — rear: wishbones/coil springs; **brakes:** front: ventilated discs — rear: ventilated discs; **wheelbase** (mm): 2,550.

The second series of the 12-cylinder boxer engines was introduced in 1976, with the 512 BB.

The Testarossa is no less than 1,976 mm wide.

Ferrari Testarossa

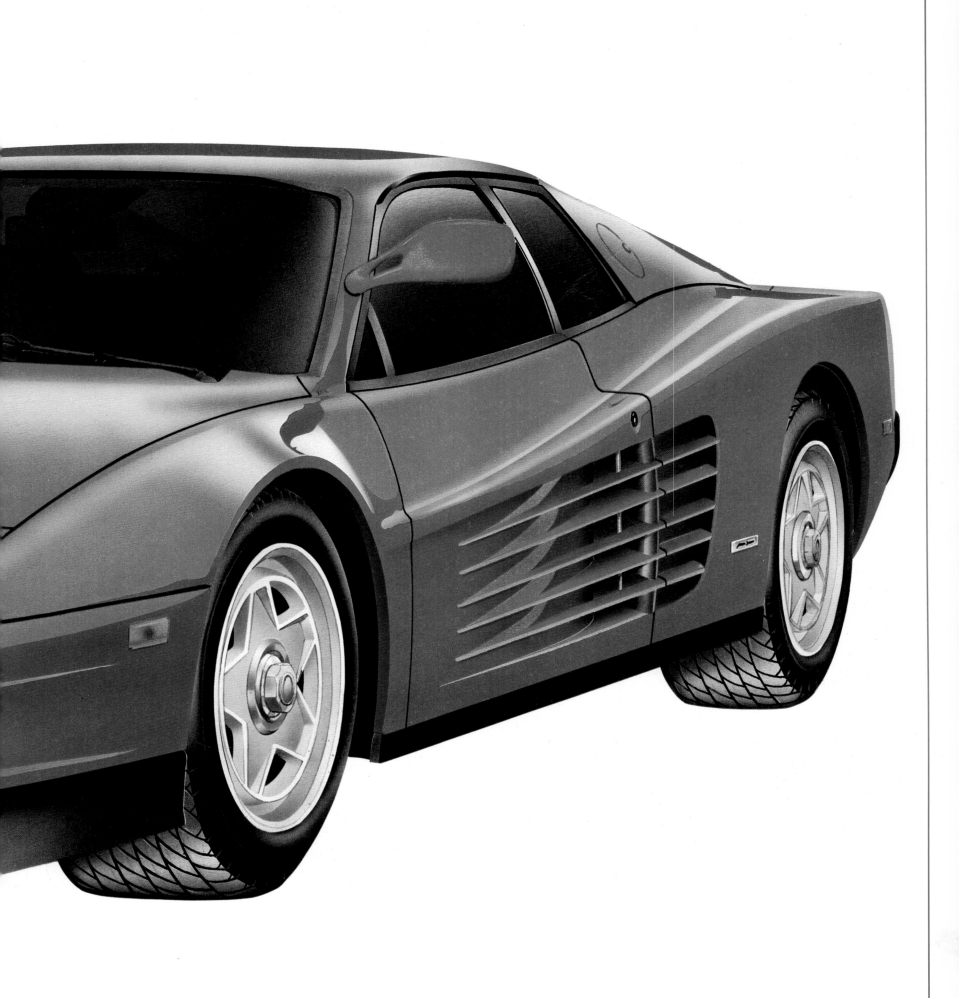

THE SPORTS-PROTOTYPES

In the immediate post-war years, at a time in which the efforts of the great automobile manufacturers were concentrated on the difficult recovery as far as series production was concerned, Enzo Ferrari made a courageous choice. At the end of 1945, he abandoned the construction of machine tools, and decided to dedicate himself entirely to sports cars. Ferrari entrusted Gioachino Colombo with designing a 1,500 cm^3 12-cylinder in-line engine following the pre-war regulations for Grand Prix cars. Once he had completed the design for the new engine, Colombo returned to Alfa Romeo, and the construction and development of the 12-V were thus carried forward by Luigi Bazzi, Attilio Galetto, and Giuseppe Busso, who made several modifications. The first car, conceived in three versions (Sport, Competizione, and Gran Premio), was ready in March 1947. Its code, 125, derived from the engine's displacement, a system that Ferrari was later to abandon only on rare occasions.

With a displacement of 1,498 cm^3, entirely in light alloy, the three carburetor racing version of the Colombo 12-V generated 118 hp at 7,000 rpm. The 125 C, a two-seater with bodywork fitted by Ferrari, made its debut on May 11, 1947, in the 1st Circuit at Piacenza, where Cortesi was forced to withdraw while in the lead. The first victory occurred on the Rome circuit of Caracalla on May 25th, once again with Cortesi at the wheel. In August 1947, the 125 was immediately replaced by the 159 S, and the following year by the 166 series. With one of these cars, christened simply 166 and provided with coupé bodywork by Allemano, Biondetti won the 1948 Mille Miglia. The following year, the version intended for Sport races was the new 166 MM. With Touring Superleggera spider bodywork, this car, which generated 140 hp at 6,600 rpm, could boast victories in the Targa Florio and Mille Miglia driven by Biondetti and, above all, in the Le Mans 24-Hour driven by Chinetti and Selsdon.

For the 1950 season, the Maranello-built Sports cars were subjected to an evolution at various levels. Firstly, Colombo's 12-V was further developed in the 195 S version, which flanked the still successful 166 MM. Moreover, with the arrival of Aurelio Lampredi, the first Sports cars fitted with his "long" 12-V engine were entered in races. These were the 275 Ss, in which the 3.3-liter engine of the 275 F1 generated a reduced power of 270 hp. The two 195 S that were built were fitted with Touring bodywork, one of them winning a victory in the Mille Miglia with Gianni Marzotto at the wheel. The 275 S, entered in the same race with almost identical bodywork, were not used again in races and were fitted with the 340 America's 4.1 liter engine at the end of the year.

The following season, the further re-boring of the Colombo engine led to the development of the 2,562 cm^3 212 Export. With a Touring bodywork, this car obtained a victory in the Tour de France with Pierre Boncompagni (known as "Pagnibon") at the wheel, while a version with Vignale coupé bodywork driven by Taruffi and Chinetti took first place in the II Carrera Panamericana. Villoresi's 340 America coupé gained Ferrari its fourth consecutive victory in the Mille·Miglia.

In 1952, following the intermediate 225 S version, the short 12-V was used for the first time with the "classic" displacement of 2,953 cm^3 which characterized the new 250 S. It was in fact this car which won the Mille Miglia, driven by Bracco and Rolfo. In addition to the 250, on various occasions Ferrari also entered an experimental 4.1-liter car with Vignale spider and coupé bodywork. Three 340 Mexico with bodywork by Vignale were entered in the Carrera Panamericana.

The 1953 racing season saw the introduction of the Manufacturer's World Championship limited to Sports cars. The Italian company's 12-cylinder weapons were the MM 166 II series, 250 and 340, and the new 4.5-liter 375. The 3 and 4.1 liters, with 240 and 280 hp respectively, had aggressive bodywork designed by Pininfarina, or, alternatively, appeared in the famous Vignale spider bodywork which also equipped many 166s. Of the six championship races, Ferrari won the Mille Miglia with the Vignale 340 MM driven by Gianni Marzotto, the Spa 24-Hour with the 4.5-liter driven by Hawthorn and Farina, and the Nürburgring 1,000-km race with the 4.5-liter Vignale driven by Ascari and Farina. The Ferrari thus won the prized title in the category.

In 1954, the development of the 4.5-liter gave rise to the 375 MM provided with saloon or spider bodywork, both by Pininfarina. In addition to this car, intended specifically for a sports-loving clientele, Ferrari also raced the 375 Plus. The victories which the Plus obtained at Buenos Aires with Farina/Maglioli, at Le Mans with Gonzales/Trintignant, and in the Carrera Panamericana with Maglioli earned Ferrari its second world title.

In 1955, Ferrari concentrated its energies on the 4-cylinder 626 and 750 Monza with which its collaboration with the Scaglietti body-makers began. Occasionally, the new 118 LM with 3,747 cm^3 6-cylinder in-line engine were also used. This car was replaced by the 121 LM, with a displacement of 4,412 cm^3 and 6-cylinder, capable of generating 330 hp. Nevertheless, the season was not a successful one, with the world title going to Mercedes. A subsequent version, the 3,431 cm^3 860 Monza, appeared in the Tourist Trophy, and, at the beginning of the following year, it took first and second place in the Sebring 12-Hour race, driven by the crews composed of Fangio/Castellotti and Musso/Schell. The 860 was the last car to be developed by Aurelio Lampredi, who was replaced toward the end of 1956, by a staff consisting

of Jano, Massimino, Bellentani, and Fraschetti.

The new season marked Ferrari's return to the 12-cylinder, initially with the 410 S with the Superamerica GT's 4,961 cm^3 engine entered solely in the first race of the season in Buenos Aires, and then with the new 290 MM. Fitted with Scaglietti bodywork similar to that of the 860 Monza and without any substantial innovations in the mechanical layout, this car was equipped with a 3,490 cm^3 12-cylinder with 2 valves per cylinder with one camshaft per bank of cylinders. This engine, capable of generating 320 hp, was almost entirely new, in that it had cylinder liners screwed to the head typical of the Colombo 12-V with new size bore and stroke and new combustion chambers. Once again, Ferrari won the Manufacturer's Championship, thanks to results such as the Castellotti's success in the Mille Miglia with the 290 MM. At Le Mans the organizers imposed a limit of 2.5 liters for models produced in less than 100 thus causing the 24-Hour to lose its validity at an international level. For this race Ferrari prepared the 625 LM, provided with the 225 hp 2,498 cm^3 engine mounted on a Testa Rossa chassis, which finished in third place driven by Gendebien/Trintignant.

In 1957 the 290 MM was developed into the 290 S provided with twin camshaft timing which increased the power to 350 hp. The displacement was further increased in the 3,783 cm^3 315 S version and in the 4,023 cm^3 335 S. In the Mille Miglia, De Portago's 335 S was involved in a tragic accident 25 miles (40 km) from the finish line which cost the driver his life, and also that of his codriver and 10 spectators, clouding the victory won by Piero Taruffi's 315 S and marking the end of the famous road race. In the next race at the Nürburgring, the 335 S driven by Collins and Gendebien was classified in second place, while the only Ferrari to finish in the Le Mans race was the 315 S driven by Lewis-Evans and Severi, who were classified in fifth place.

In 1956 and 1957, the Testa Rossa had started to obtain favorable results in the under 2-liter category, initially with the 500 TR and TRC 4-cylinder versions, and then with the 250 TR 12-cylinder version. In 1958, the new displacement limit of 3 liters was introduced, allowing the latter, in various official versions as well as those for clients, to take the Manufacturer's Championship title in 1958, 1960 and 1961. In 1962, the Championship was limited to Grand Tourers, and Ferrari did not fail to win it, thanks to the results of the 250 GTO. However, at the same time, development of the Sports-Prototypes also continued. Between 1958 and 1960, the company had already raced several Sports fitted with 6-cylinder V Dino engines mounted in a rear position. In 1961 and 1962, the new SP series was used to replace the Testa Rossa on the official team. These cars were not very successful, despite their sophisticated technical characteristics, and Ferrari continued to obtain the best results with the 12-cylinder which won the Le Mans 24-Hour in 1961 and 1962.

Starting in 1963, the P-P4 series Sports-Prototypes entered competition, and were involved in a heated battle with Ford between 1964 and 1967. Directly derived from the 250 P the 250 Le Mans was proved to be highly satisfactory to sports-loving clients until 1967, and also succeeded in winning the Le Mans race in 1965. At the end of 1967, the sudden change in the regulations, that created two separate categories for 3-liter Prototypes and 5-liter Sports, meant that Ferrari could no longer use the still competitive 330 P4s and withdrew from the 1968 season. In 1969, the Maranello company returned to the category once again with the 312 P Prototype, fitted with the same 2,989 cm^3 engine as the 312 F1. Compared to the single-seater, its power was only slightly reduced, reaching 420 hp at 9,800 rpm. For the chassis, the company adopted the classic mixed tubular structure reinforced by panels. The car immediately proved to be competitive, although its potential was hampered above all by problems concerning reliability and fuel consumption. The 312 Ps were not used in the two final races of the Championship, which was won by Porsche, and passed to NART the following season. The 3-liter Ferrari was then modified with an original spider bodywork with which it raced until 1974.

In 1970, Ferrari decided to concentrate on the new 5-liter 512 S, abandoning the 3-liter Prototypes which stood no chance of success against the more powerful and equally sophisticated Sports. Despite Giunti/Vaccarella/Andretti's win at Sebring, the large Ferraris did not manage to pose a threat to the Porsche 917s, which gained the title. In Austria, in the last race in the Championship program, the more competitive 512 M was entered. However, in 1971 the management of this car was left entirely to the private teams, as the official team had decided to concentrate exclusively on the development of the new 312 P Prototype with boxer engine. The new 3-liter won in 1972 the Championship with 10 victories in 10 races.

However, in 1973, the 312 Ps were defeated by the Matra-Simcas, before Ferrari's definitive withdrawal from the category. Nevertheless, the tradition of building high performance sophisticated cars in order to satisfy the demands of a sports-loving clientele, was taken up once more in 1984, with a series of cars which embodied the same "spirit." However, due to the decline of the Manufacturer's Championship and considering the lack of contests suitable for cars of this type, the 1984 GTO and the subsequent F40 of 1987 have not been able to prove themselves on the track, becoming mere collector's items in too brief a space of time.

250 TESTA ROSSA

The first Ferrari to go by the name of Testa Rossa due to the color of its head covers which marked since 1954 the most effective engines in terms of horsepower, was the 500 TR of 1956. It was fitted with the 1,985 cm³ 4-cylinder engine that had equipped the Mondial series. Available in two versions with different bodywork, one built by Touring and the other by Scaglietti with a Pininfarina design, this car was followed a year later by the 500 TRC.

For the 1958 season, the engine capacity of the Sports that were to contend for the Manufacturer's Championship was to be limited to 3 liters. Ferrari's technical staff, directed by Andrea Fraschetti, thus decided to develop a new vehicle that could be marketed with success among European and American sports-loving clients. The project was based on the 2,953 cm³ 12-V single camshaft engine of the 250 GT, and the first prototype was entered at the Nürburgring in 1957, and in the Swedish Grand Prix for Sports cars. It was a 290 MM onto which the new engine was fitted, with a ladder frame chassis and De Dion rear axle with transverse leaf springs. A second prototype, this time with the chassis of the 500 TRC, composed of tubes with various sections, was prepared for Le Mans with an engine capacity increased to 3,117 cm³ solely for this occasion. It had wishbone suspension in front with coil springs and rear suspension consisting of a rigid axle anchored by trailing radius arms with lever dampers. The bodywork, designed and built by Scaglietti, adopted the characteristic openings between the nose and mudguards in order to cool the large drums at the front. This car anticipated the definitive version for the clientele which was presented at Modena on November 22. The Testa Rossas entered directly by the company in 1958 (designated TR/58) differed from the version available to clients in that they had De Dion rear axles instead of rigid axles. The engine generated 290 hp at 7,500 rpm.

In the course of the season, during which Carlo Chiti replaced Fraschetti as technical manager, the official team also prepared some experimental cars. One of these possessed a 2,962 cm³ Dino 6-V engine, that was immediately replaced by the 12-cylinder. In the search for an optimum weight distribution, the gearbox was placed in unit with the differential in two cars.

The 1958 season came to an end with Ferrari winning the Manufacturer's Championship thanks to the successful results obtained by the TR/58 driven by Hill and Collins in Argentina, at Sebring and in the Targa Florio, as well as by Hill and Gendebien at Le Mans. After this race, one of the company's Testa Rossas received Dunlop disc brakes and had its bodywork updated. This changes preceded modifications that were to be adopted a year later. Production of the "client" version ceased in 1958.

The TR/59, which had its first run on the Modena circuit in January, had new bodywork designed by Pininfarina and built by Fantuzzi. Mechanically, apart from the disc brakes, the basic innovations lay in the new 5-speed magnesium gearbox, a lighter chassis, and telescopic dampers instead of lever dampers. The engine, thanks to a new valve control with coil springs, could safely reach 8,700 rpm. Despite the good omen provided by the victory won by Gurney/Daigh/Hill/Gendebien at Sebring, Ferrari subsequently did not manage to achieve any further successes, leaving the world title in the hands of Aston Martin. Following problems with the engines at Le Mans, Chiti decided to adopt a dry sump lubrication system, used for the first time in the Tourist Trophy.

In 1960, the same cars from the previous year were used initially, conforming with the new regulations which, among other things, demanded a higher windscreen. The wheelbase was also slightly shortened to respect the minimum steering diameter imposed by the organizers of the Le Mans 24-Hour. Initially, in place of the much criticized 5-speed gearbox, a 4-speed transaxle gear-

Of the 30 Testa Rossas produced in all, 19 were 250 TRs, the version meant for the company's clientele.

box was adopted, although it was subsequently abandoned after being tested in a 5-speed version. In March, two new cars, christened TR/60, were built and entered in the Le Mans race. These cars had the engine and gearbox unit mounted in a slightly further back position and had independent rear suspension with double trailing arms almost identical to those used on the F.1 single-seater. The two victories obtained by the TR/60 at Buenos Aires and Le Mans, respectively driven by Hill/Allison and Gendebien/Frère, permitted Ferrari to take the world title.

In 1961, despite the parallel development of the new rear-engined prototypes, the Testa Rossa underwent a through revision, with a new and lighter space frame that was much more rigid than the previous one and with four wheel independent suspension consisting of trailing arms. The engine was mounted in a still lower as well as further back position. However, it was the bodywork in particular that was new, with the arrow-shaped nose typical of Ferrari at the time and a high tail fitted with a spoiler. Hill and Gendebien won at Sebring and Le Mans, while Bandini and Scarfiotti shared the winning car at Pescara. The Maranello company won the Manufacturer's Championship, which was to be restricted to GTs the following year. Nevertheless, the TR/61 was also driven with success the next season, gaining a victory at Sebring with Bianchi and Bonnier. The car's swan song occurred in the form a victory for Hill and Gendebien at Le Mans, at the wheel of a new version specially built for the occasion, the 330 TRI. It was rather a heterogeneous mixture of Ferrari components. The chassis was of the TR/61 type, with a longer wheelbase and rear brakes on the differential. The 3,967 cm³ engine was derived from that of the Superamerica. Fed by six twin barrel carburetors, it generated 360 hp at 7,200 rpm.

The Testa Rossa's career came to an end in 1963. A total of 30 Testa Rossas were completed in all: two prototypes, two TR/58s, 19 250 TRs, four TR/60s, two TR/61s, and one 330 TRI.

Technical data

MODEL 250 TESTA ROSSA (TR/59)
YEAR OF PRODUCTION 1959

ENGINE
position: front longitudinal; **cylinders:** 60° 12V-cm³ 2,953; **compression:** 9,8:1; **feed:** 6 Weber 40DCN carburators; **ignition:** single; **timing:** 2 valves per cylinder-1 OHC per bank chain driven; **max power:** 225 kW (306 hp) at 7,400 rpm.

CHASSIS
gearbox: 5-speed + reverse; **suspensions:** front: wishbones/coil springs — rear: De Dion axle/coil springs; **brakes:** front: discs — rear: discs; **wheelbase** (mm): 2,350.

Ferrari 250 Testa Rossa (TR/59)

Ferrari 246 SP

246 SP

1961 proved to be fundamental year in the history of Ferrari racing cars. In fact, in February, the new mid-engine cars were presented, that is to say the 156 F1 and 246 SP Sport. The latter had a tubular space frame with a rear cradle of triangular section tubes in which the engine was located and which also supported the suspensions. As far as these were concerned, there was independent suspension both in the front and the rear with coil springs and telescopic damper struts. The rear disc brakes were placed at the exit of the differential. The two fuel tanks were inserted into the vehicle's sides, while the water and oil coolers were situated in the nose.

The engine belonged to the Dino family and was a 65° 6-cylinder V. It was entirely made of light alloy and possessed dry sump lubrication. Fed by three twin barrel carburetors and fitted with twin camshaft timing, it could generate 270 hp at 8,000 rpm, approximately 25 hp more than the 1958 F1 version. There was a 5-speed gearbox.

The extremely advanced and compact bodywork was adapted after it was given a faired headrest with a Jaguar D type fin and, once again on the bonnet, a transparent air inlet. All of these features were not present when the definitive version made its racing debut. This occurred in the Sebring 12-Hour, with a car driven by von Trips and Ginther. The new 6-cylinder Sport's first victory occurred in the next World Championship race, the Targa Florio, in which two 246 SPs were entered. One was driven by Hill/Gendebien and the other by von Trips/Ginther. After Hill's car left the track, the Belgian driver took Ginther's place beside von Trips, and managed to be first over the finish line. This occurred after the Porsche, which was leading the race, was betrayed by transmission problems four miles from the end. In 1961, there were no further victories for the rear-engine Ferrari cars. However, it should be stressed that Ginther and Baghetti's 246 SP was well in the lead in the Le Mans 24-Hour, when they were forced to withdraw due to the Italian driver leaving the track.

On February 24, 1962, during the traditional beginning of the season press conference, the revised versions of the Sports-Prototypes were presented with the new GTO. These cars had identical bodywork. They differed from those of the previous year above all in the lower bonnet, aligned with the lower windscreen that was in conformity with the new regulations, although the four cars were fitted with different engines. The 196 SP and the 286 SP adopted the 60° 6-cylinder V in the version with single camshaft and dry sump lubrication. They possessed engine capacities of 1,984 cm³ and 2,868 cm³, and 200 hp at 7,800 rpm and 260 hp at 6,800 rpm, respectively. From a mechanical point of view, the 246 SP remained unchanged. The choice of engine for the

248 SP was entirely without precedent, the car being fitted with the 90° 8-cylinder V designed by Chiti a year earlier on the basis of the engine inherited from Lancia. This motor, provided with wet sump lubrication, had a displacement of 2,458 cm³, which was almost immediately increased to 2,645 cm³. At the same time, dry sump lubrication was adopted by the 268 SP. The new 8-V's original characteristics included four twin barrel carburetors inserted directly into the head, without the interposition of the traditional manifolds.

The 246 SP was entered on all occasions on which the official Ferrari team was present. It won the Targa Florio with Rodriguez/Mairesse/Gendebien at the wheel and also at the Nürburgring with Hill/Gendebien. The 248 SP was used solely at Sebring, where the American crew Fulp and Ryan took 13th place. The subsequent 268 SP version obtained several useful results, although it was in the limelight at Le Mans, where Baghetti and Scarfiotti were forced to withdraw after 21 hours while in third place. The regulations particular to the French race induced all the SPs to adopt a higher windscreen, which was matched with a rear roll-bar to redress the car's aerodynamic balance. The little 196 SP took second place in the Targa Florio driven by Baghetti and Bandini. However it found its true strong point in climbing races, winning the European Mountain Championship (driven by Scarfiotti).

In 1963 and 1964, the Ferrari SPs, fitted with new noses similar to those of the new 250 P, distinguished themselves once more in endurance and climbing races, driven primarily by the private teams. They were officially entered in the 1963 Targa Florio, in which Bandini, Scarfiotti and Mairesse's 196 SP came in second place, after having led for much of the race.

In conclusion, the SP series cars proved to be extremely fast, although unsuitable for endurance races. Ferrari had continued to obtain the best results in these contests with the 12-Vs with forward engines.

Technical data

MODEL 246 SP
YEAR OF PRODUCTION 1961-1962

ENGINE
position: rear central longitudinal; **cylinders:** 65° 6V-cm³ 2,417; **compression:** 9,8:1; **feed:** 3 Weber 42DCN carburetors; **ignition:** dual; **timing:** 2 valves per cylinder-2 OHC per bank chain driven; **max power:** 198 kW (270 hp) at 8,000 rpm.

CHASSIS
gearbox: 5 speed + reverse; **suspensions:** front: wishbones/coil springs — rear: wishbones/coil springs; **brakes:** front: discs — rear: discs; **wheelbase** (mm): 2,320.

The 246 SP was presented on the Modena circuit on February 13, 1961, with a showy rear fin that was later abandoned.

250 GTO

In 1964, Graham Hill won the Sussex Trophy at Goodwood at the wheel of a GTO belonging to the "Maranello Limited" team.

In the summer of 1960, in view of the new regulations that two years later were to restrict the Manufacturer's World Championship to the GT category, Enzo Ferrari entrusted Bizzarrini with the creation of a new car, which underwent a series of tests in the prototype stage on the Monza track in September. It was a berlinetta, for which the name 250 GT Competizione was chosen. This, according to the most commonly quoted anecdotes, became GTO (the "O" standing for *Omologata* - Homologated) due to a typing error made in the FIA's offices. The tubular space frame of the short wheelbase 250 GT was chosen as the basis for its development, and was modified mainly in the engine lower rear position, and in the addition of several cross members to increase rigidity. The mountings of the front suspension were also modified. The disc brakes had light alloy calipers and their diameter was greater than those of the 250 GT. The bodywork, unusually designed by the Maranello company itself, was produced entirely in aluminum by Scaglietti. The side louvers on the front mudguards were typical, one serving to disperse the heat produced by the brakes and tires and the other (or two in some cases) for the expulsion of hot air from the engine compartment. The nose was characterized by three small air inlets that were protected by special caps which served the purpose of increasing the air flow towards the cooler in the case of high external temperatures.

The light alloy engine was the same 2,953 cm³ 12-V that equipped the GT version. The only difference between them was the adoption of dry sump lubrication. The timing was single camshaft with two 35° V valves, while the feed was entrusted to six twin barrel carburetors mounted as usual between the two banks of cylinders. The power generated reached 290 hp at 7,400 rpm.

The GTO had a 5-speed Porsche type synchromesh gearbox, while the limited slip differential was built by Ferrari itself on license from the German ZF. In order to adapt the vehicle to every circuit, eight different axle ratios were available, allowing for a maximum speed range of 126 mph (203 km/h) to 175 mph (283 km/h).

In 1962, three GTOs, fitted with the 3,967 cm³ engine with three carburetors used on the 400 Superamerica were also prepared. In one of these cars Parkes and Mairesse took second place in the 1,000-km race at the Nürburgring. The 4-liter version, also entered unsuccessfully at Le Mans with a six-carburetor feed, constituted the basis for the development of the 330 GT of 1963.

The GTO's racing debut took place on March 24, 1962, in the Sebring 12-Hour, in which the crew composed of Phil Hill and Gendebien finished in second place. Another excellent result was second place outright in the Le Mans 24-Hour, with Noblet and Guichet at the wheel. There were numerous victories in the GT category, while other outright victories to be remembered include those obtained by Guichet and Behra in the 1963 Tour de France, and the 1962 and 1963 Tourist Trophies, won by Innes Ireland and Graham Hill respectively. In 1964, the final year of the GTO's career, a new 3-liter version was built, having the same chassis as the previous version. A fundamental innovation was the new bodywork, designed by Pininfarina. It was lower and wider, and characterized by a vertical rear window which repeated the aesthetics of the prototypes (with rear engine) introduced the year before. The tracks were widened, as was the section of the tires. There was a new ratios for the 5-speed gearbox, and the brake system was improved through the use of twin pumps. Three GTOs were originally built in this form. Another four were obtained by putting new bodies on 1962 models. The GTO was the last great Ferrari racing car with front engine; 39 were built in all.

Technical data

MODEL 250 GTO	
YEAR OF PRODUCTION 1964-1966	

ENGINE
position: front longitudinal; **cylinders:** 60° 12V-cm³ 2,953; **compression:** 9,8:1; **feed:** 6 Weber 38DCN carburetors; **ignition:** single; **timing:** 2 valves per cylinder-1 OHC per bank chain driven; **max power:** 213 kW (290 hp) at 7,400 rpm.

CHASSIS
gearbox: 5-speed + reverse; **suspensions:** front: wishbones/coil springs — rear: rigid axle/longitudinal leaf springs; **brakes:** front: discs — rear: discs; **wheelbase** (mm): 2,490.

The 250 GTO driven by Beurlys and Langlois took second place overall in the 1963 Le Mans 24-Hour.

Ferrari 250 GTO

Ferrari 250 Le Mans

250-330 P / 250 LE MANS

The 250 Le Mans with 3-liter engine presented at the Paris Show of 1963.

As a successor to the GTO in the Grand Tourers category, Ferrari decided to create a project directly derived from the "P" series prototypes with rear engine introduced in 1963, which had proved to be an immediate success. In March of that year, the 250 P was presented at Monza, with bodywork designed by Pininfarina mounted on a tubular space frame with four wheel independent suspensions, adopting the by then well-tested pattern of upper and lower wishbones. The engine remained the powerful 2,953 cm^3 12-V of the Testa Rossa, fed by six twin barrel carburetors and capable of generating 300 hp at 7,800 rpm. The non-synchronized 5-speed gearbox was placed outboard behind the transaxle assembly with the brakes in board at the exit of the differential.

The 1963 season proved to be rich in successes for the 250 P, of which four were built. The first victory was gained in the Sebring 12-Hour by Surtees/Scarfiotti, who were followed by an identical car driven by Mairesse/Vaccarella.

After an unsuccessful Targa Florio, the new prototype won the Nürburgring 1,000-km, driven by Surtees and Mairesse. From this race onward, the clutch was no longer placed near the flywheel, but behind the gearbox. At Le Mans Bandini and Scarfiotti's 250 P was first over the finish line. Towards the end of the season, the new 330 P made its debut. This car was structurally identical, but fitted with the 3,967 cm^3 Superamerica engine generating 370 hp at 7,300 rpm. In 1964, this model was adopted by the official team together with the 275P, in which the 3-liter engine was increased to 3,286 cm^3 thanks to a larger bore. The power also increased to 320 hp at 7,500 rpm. The car's shape was slightly altered for the new season, with the nose and tail being lengthened and the windscreen and roll-bar behind the cockpit being redesigned. Three different chassis were built with this new form,

all of which could adopt, depending on the circumstances, either the 3-liter of 3.3-liter engine. The latter was also installed in the four 1963 version cars.

In the meantime, the 250 LM (with a body that was in practice a coupé version of these prototypes), retaining the same mechanical layout apart from the clutch, which was once again situated behind the flywheel, had been presented at the Paris Show in October, 1963. With this car, Ferrari aimed to obtain the CSI rating in the Grand Tourers class. However, this was not granted, forcing the new Le Mans to compete in the prototype category too, compromising its commercial chances as far as the company's traditional sports-loving clientele was concerned.

Apart from the first cars, fitted with the 3-liter engine, the remaining 31 250 LMs (which never assumed the "275" code) built between 1964 and 1965, adopted the 3.3-liter engine. The shape was also slightly modified immediately. The results included a smooth roof that no longer had the typical rear tapering which left a fissure between the roof and the roll-bar structure and a bonnet that more closely resembled that of the prototypes. The 1964 season was characterized by numerous successes for the 275 P, including Scarfiotti and Vaccarella's victory at Sebring, and that of Guichet and Vaccarella at Le Mans. The 330 P obtained its first victory in the Tourist Trophy, with Graham Hill at the wheel, followed by that in the Paris 1,000-km (G. Hill-Bonnier) and in the Bettoja Trophy at Monza driven by Scarfiotti. As for the 250 LM, which ran for the semi-official teams, the first 3-liter car, entered by NART, crashed at Sebring. Its first important result was fifth place at the Nürburgring, while its first victory was in the Reims 12-Hour won by G. Hill and Bonnier. This was followed by Piper and Maggs' win in the Kyalami 9-Hour.

In 1965, while the prototypes made way for the new P2, the 250 LM's sporting career successfully continued. Mairesse won the Coupes de Belgique at Zolder, later repeating this victory in the Spa 500-km. However, the most important result was the victory in the Le Mans 24-Hour, won by Masten Gregory and Jochen Rindt behind the wheel of a NART 250 LM. Even more incredible was the fact that an identical vehicle, belonging to the Francorchamps team and driven by Dumay and Gosselin, took second place.

In 1965, Pininfarina also built a "fast-back" version of the 250 LM exclusively for use on the road (similar to that which had appeared as an experiment in the preliminary trials for the 1964 Le Mans race) with a more carefully finished interior and left-hand drive. Very few of these cars were built. The 250 remained among the protagonists of endurance racing for a long period. Proof of this can be seen in the victory won by Parkes and Piper in the Paris 1,000-km in 1966, and fifth place in the 1,000-km race at Brands Hatch, obtained by Rodriguez and Pierpoint in 1968. Piper and Attwood obtained seventh place at Le Mans in the same year.

The "fast-back" bodywork offered by Pininfarina in 1965.

Technical data

MODEL 250 LM
YEAR OF PRODUCTION 1963-1966

ENGINE
position: rear central longitudinal; **cylinders:** 60° 12V-cm^3 3,286 (2,953); **compression:** 9,8:1; **feed:** 6 Weber 38 DCN carburetors; **ignition:** single; **timing:** 2 valves per cylinder-1 OHC per bank chain driven; **max power:** 235 kW (320 hp) at 7,500 rpm (221 kW/300 hp at 7,500 rpm).

CHASSIS
gearbox: 5-speed + reverse; **suspensions:** front: wishbones/coil springs — rear: wishbones/coil springs; **brakes:** front: discs — rear: discs; **wheelbase** (mm): 2,400.

(the figures in brackets refer to the 1963 3-liter).

275-330 P2 / 330 P3-P4

The offensive launched by Ford in 1964 against Ferrari was successfully resisted by the Maranello company with its own P series Sports. The fact that the Detroit-based company continued to insist on undermining Modena in the role of capital of the fastest racing cars (which took the form of cars with increasingly high engine capacities) was met by Ferrari's creating a series of particularly sophisticated Prototypes.

Thus, in 1965, the P2 came into being, in the 275 and 330 variants. The influence of the single-seater was already apparent in the chassis, with the adoption of a "semi-monocoque," configuration used for the first time on the 156 F1. The rear suspensions also derived from those used on the Grand Prix cars, with a parallelogram pattern consisting of a single upper transverse arm and a lower wishbone, integrated by two trailing radius arms. This structure made it possible to exploit fully the new Dunlop tires with particularly wide section, for which the Borrani wire wheels were also replaced by new magnesium alloy rims. The evolution of the "long" 60° 12-cylinder engine was also significant, with the adoption of twin camshaft timing and dual ignition. Two spark plugs placed inside the rows of cylinders. The feed was once again entrusted to six twin barrel carburetors. The engine was available with a displacement of 3,285 and 3,967 cm³ and could generate 350 hp at 8,500 rpm and 410 hp at 8,200 rpm, respectively. The gearbox, in block with the differential, was 5-speed.

The spider bodywork, built by Fantuzzi, was presented in December 1964, with a low windscreen but without aerodynamic roll-bar. The latter was adopted in February of the following year, together with a larger windscreen, in conformity with the European regulations for the "Prototypes" category. Its racing debut took place at Daytona, where the 330 P2 driven by Surtees and Rodriguez, which was fitted with a low windscreen and simple tubular roll-bar for the occasion, was forced to withdraw. The first victory was that obtained at Monza by the 275 P2 driven by Parkes and Guichet, followed in second place by the 330 P2 with Surtees and Scarfiotti at the wheel. In the same race, Filipinetti entered the first of the new 365 P prototypes, intended for the semi-official teams. Based on the same chassis as the P2, it was however provided with a 4,390 cm³ engine with single camshaft timing and ignition. It generated 380 hp at 7,300 rpm. The Targa Florio was the scene of another success for the 275 P2, driven by Bandini and Vaccarella, followed by the victory at the Nürburgring won by the 330 P2 entrusted to Surtees and Scarfiotti, who led the race for its entire 1,000 km duration. After the P2s had outclassed all rivals in the trials which took place in April, at Le Mans all the official Ferrari prototypes were forced to withdraw, leaving the first two places in the final classification to two 250 LMs. In the French 24-Hour, the 275 P2 driven by Bandini and Biscaldi was entered with new, closed bodywork. The Reims 12-Hour, the last important race of the season, was won by Rodriguez and Guichet's 365 P. With a similar car, Piper and Attwood ended the season by winning the Kyalami 9-Hour.

For the 1966 season, in reply to Ford's 7-liter cars, Ferrari maintained its new 330 P3 below the 4-liter limit, counting on the car's qualities as far as lightness and maneuverability were concerned. However, the power was increased to 420 hp at 8,000 rpm thanks to te adoption of a Lucas injection system.

A new ZF gearbox was also used, with the clutch no longer being situated below the final transmission, but more conventionally between the engine and the gearbox. The bodywork now had a much more modern closed shape designed by Piero Drogo's Sports Car company. This season, during which Ferrari was plagued by notable problems with the unions, once again revolved around the duel with Ford, which won the first two races at Daytona, where the Italian company did not participate, and at

The 330 P2 driven by Surtees and Scarfiotti that won the Nürburgring 1,000-km race in 1965.

Sebring, where Parkes and Bondurant's 330 P3 was forced to withdraw. The Ferraris vindicated themselves at Monza and Spa, won respectively by Surtees/Parkes and Scarfiotti/Parkes, while at the Nürburgring, the only P3, driven by Surtees/Parkes, withdrew, leaving Chaparral to claim the victory. At Le Mans, the race went in Ford's favor due to an incredible series of withdrawals on the part of the Maranello cars, which nevertheless won the Manufacturer's Championship. In December, 1966, the new 330 P4 made its appearance in a series of tests on the Daytona circuit. Despite the fact that it had bodywork similar to that of the P3, it was actually the result of an almost entirely new project. The 4-liter engine was radically modified by Franco Rocchi, who obtained a power of 450 hp at 8,000 rpm adopting a three valve head per cylinder. The monoblock was reinforced, while the injection inlets placed between the two cylinder banks were new. The ZF gearbox was abandoned in favor of a 6-speed "homemade" one. The P3s of the previous year were reconverted into the new 412 P intended for clients, fitted with heads with two valves per cylinder and carburetor feed.

For the P4, the season began with a memorable victory at Daytona, where the spider driven by Bandini/Amon and the coupé driven by Parkes/Scarfiotti crossed the finish line in first and second place while the 412 P driven by Rodriguez/Guichet took third place. The same crew that occupied the two highest steps on the podium at Daytona repeated the result at Monza. In the Belgian race at Spa, Ferrari was forced to give up the victory to Mirage-Ford, obtaining only a third place with Bianchi/Attwood's 412 P. At Le Mans yet another battle took place with Ford, whose 7-liter gained the upper hand. The two P4s driven by Parkes/Scarfiotti and Mairesse/Beurlys finished in second and third place. Later, Ferrari also gained a second place at Brands Hatch with Amon and Stewart coming in after the victorious Chaparral, winning the Manufacturer's Championship yet again.

Technical data

MODEL 330 P4
YEAR OF PRODUCTION 1967

ENGINE
position: rear central longitudinal; **cylinders:** 60° 12V-cm³ 3,967; **compression:** 11,0:1; **feed:** Lucas mechanical injection; **ignition:** dual; **timing:** 3 valves per cylinder-2 OCH per bank chain driven; **max power:** 331 kW (450 hp) at 8,000 rpm.

CHASSIS
gearbox: 5-speed + reverse; **suspensions:** front: wishbones/coil springs — rear: wishbones/coil springs; **brakes:** front: discs — rear: discs; **wheelbase** (mm): 2,400.

Ferrari 330 P4

Ferrari 512 M

512 S / 512 M

The 1970 Manufacturer's World Championship promised to be an exciting challenge for the powerful 5-liter Sports cars, a category in which Porsche had already entered its 917 the previous year. Ferrari had not presented its 512 S until November 1969, following a period of complex company problems that had led to Fiat acquiring a 50 percent share. In this atmosphere Forghieri hurriedly developed a new car, without being able to perfect the extremely valid basic project with the necessary care, especially from the point of view of its aerodynamics. Structurally, the 512 S had a tubular spaceframe reinforced with aluminum panels, a longitudinal central engine with ''outboard'' cantilever gearbox, lateral water-coolers located in front of the rear wheels, and oil coolers in the front. The suspension system consisted of double wishbones both in the front and the rear with coil springs and damper struts. The braking system consisted of four disc brakes placed on the wheels. The light alloy engine with cast iron cylinder liners was a 60° V-12 with dry sump lubrication and an engine capacity of 4,994 cm³. The timing consisted of chain-driven twin camshafts with four valves per cylinder, while the feed was entrusted to a Lucas mechanical injection system. The power generated 550 hp at 8,500 rpm. The bodywork was built in two versions, coupé and spider, and these were joined by a long-tailed coupé for the Le Mans 24-Hour.

The 512 S made its debut in the Daytona 24-Hour, a race in which of the five cars entered, only those of the Andretti, Ickx and Merzario crew crossed the finish line, in third place. The best result of the season was to be obtained in the subsequent Sebring 12-Hour race, with a victory for Andretti, who had been forced to withdraw while in the lead with a spider (that he shared with Merzario) taking the last turn at the wheel in the coupé driven by Giunti and Vaccarella to become the first over the finish line. Following this result, the 512s did not manage to achieve more than the two second places gained at Monza by Giunti, Vaccarella, and Amon, and at Spa by Ickx and Surtees.

In the Zeltweg 1,000-km race, Ferrari presented a substantially modified version of its own 5-liter Sport, christened 512 M, which remedied the defects of the previous version. The most significant modifications concerned the aerodynamics, with a redesigned tail and a lower nose section for a higher downforce. The latter was obtained by moving the spare tire, which was located between the two oil coolers, in the rear over the gearbox, and placing the coolers themselves toward the center. An air scoop was also placed behind the cockpit for the engine feed. The new version, which was a short-tailed coupé, featured a single rear-view mirror. The engine generated approximately 600 hp.

An immediate improvement in performance was visible, so much so that Ickx and Giunti easily led the race on the Austrian circuit before being forced to withdraw due to problems with the electrical equipment. Victory over the rival Porsche 917s came in November, in the non-Championship Kyalami 9-Hour race for Ickx and Giunti. However, this success was destined to remain the only one achieved by a 512 M. The promise of an excellent 1971 season was in fact suppressed by Ferrari's decision not to enter its own Sport officially, leaving racing management solely to the private teams. Those which distinguished themselves included the Belgian Filipinetti, the American NART and the Spanish Montjuich. The most competitive of the 512 Ms was that entered by Roger Penske's American team, which made its debut in the 1971 Daytona 24-Hour race, coming in third place with a crew composed of Donohue and Hobbs. They also managed to lead in the initial phase of the subsequent Sebring race before various problems caused them to finish in sixth place. Penske's 512 also worthily kept the Porsche cars at bay in the Le Mans race, being forced however to withdraw after four hours, in second place, due to engine failure. Nevertheless, Posey and Adamowicz, driving the Filipinetti 512 M, took third place in the French 24-Hour race. Penske's car was also forced to withdraw from the last race of the season, at Watkins Glen, while in the lead.

In short, the 512 constituted for Ferrari a missed opportunity to seriously challenge the supremacy of the Porsche cars. It was not able to achieve its full potential due to the Maranello company chosing to dedicate its resources to the new 3-liter prototype.

Technical data

MODEL 512 M
YEAR OF PRODUCTION 1971
ENGINE   **position:** rear central longitudinal; **cylinders:** 60° 12V-cm³ 4,994; **compression:** 11,8:1; **feed:** Lucas mechanical injection; **ignition:** single; **timing:** 4 valves per cylinder-2 OHC per bank chain driven; **max power:** 449 kW (610 hp) at 9,000 rpm.
CHASSIS   **gearbox:** 5-speed + reverse; **suspensions:** front: wishbones/coil springs — rear: single upper arms, lower wishbones/coil springs; **brakes:** front: discs — rear: discs; **wheelbase** (mm): 2,400.

Giunti and Vaccarella took third place with this 512 S in the 1970 Targa Florio.

312 P

Regazzoni and Redman's 312 P finished in second place in the Buenos Aires 1,000-km, the race that opened the 1972 season.

In 1971, despite the fact that the rules still permitted powerful 5-liter Sports to take part in the Manufacturer's World Championship, Ferrari preferred to leave the private teams to manage its 512 while it concentrated on the preparation of the 3-liter prototype that was to contend for the title the following year. This was a light and compact spider which utilized a 12-cylinder boxer engine derived directly from that used in Formula One. The car was presented in December 1970, as the *Prototipo Boxer* (Boxer Prototype), although the abbreviation 312 PB never appeared in the official documentation of the company. Ferrari simply adopted the names ''312 P,'' identical to that of the 1969 prototype with 12-V engine.

It made its debut in the Buenos Aires 1,000-km race, where its remarkable speed was set against the race's tragic outcome and the accident in which Ignazio Giunti lost his life. The 312 P reappeared in the Sebring 12-Hour, in which Ickx and Regazzoni led the field until forced to retire due to transmission problems.

The transmission was conceived for Grand Prix distances and still not suitable for an endurance race. At Brands Hatch the same pair of drivers held off the much more powerful Porsche 917, in the end finishing in second place due to time lost through an accident and the subsequent box stop. At the end of the season, the small light Ferrari had led in seven of the eight races in which it had participated, without however managing to gain a victory for reasons that were more often than not merely fortuitous. The first outright success occurred in the non-Championship Kyalami 9-Hour race, with Regazzoni and Redman at the wheel. The year of track tests meant that the 312 P was already fully competitive at the beginning of the 1972 season, which resulted in a veritable triumph for the Maranello prototypes.

Compared to the previous year's version the 3-liter Ferrari had a lower nose, modifications to the suspension, and, in observance of the new rules, a weight increase from 1,291 lb to 1,434 lb (505

kg to 650 kg) due to larger diameter tubes used for the chassis.

Although its adversaries did not prove to be particularly tough, the fact that the 312 P won all ten races in which it was entered should not be undervalued. In six of them it occupied the first two places, twice the first three, and once, in Austria, even the first four. The driver who gained the greatest number of victories was Ickx, who won three together with Mario Andretti, one with Clay Regazzoni, and one with Brian Redman. Moreover, drivers such as Merzario, Peterson, Schenken, Munari, Marko and Carlos Pace also contributed to winning the Manufacturer's Championship.

The 312 P during trials for the Vallelunga 6-Hour race in 1973.

Ferrari 312 P

Compared to the Formula One, the 2,991 boxer generated less power — approximately 400 hp at 10,000 rpm — although it was more versatile, due to an excellent torque developed to start from 6,500 rpm. The chassis was built according to Ferrari's typical "semi monocoque" structure, with the engine suspended from a special rear truss. The water coolers were located on the cockpit's sides while the oil coolers were above the engine. The front suspension consisted of the traditional system of double wishbones and springs and dampers on the wheels. In the rear there was a system with upper transverse arms combined with lower wishbones. The latter was replaced at the season's end by two parallel trailing arms.

The glass fiber bodywork was split into two sections, a front one which included the two small doors, and a rear one in three variants: with a short, medium or long tail, the final version appearing solely in the preliminary trials for Le Mans (the only race in which Ferrari did not participate in 1972.) The following year, the scenario of the Manufacturer's Championship changed radically with the mass entry of Matra. For the new season, the fundamental modifications carried out on the 312 P consisted of the adoption of a longer nose without the central air inlet and an increased wheelbase, as well as the adoption of "periscope" air inlets to feed the engine. This had a bore and stroke of slightly different dimensions, rendering it more oversquared, with a power of 450-460 hp at 11,000 rpm. The change from Firestone to Goodyear tires caused notable problems for the Maranello-built cars, and vain attempts were made to reduce a chronic tendency to understeer. The 1973 season revolved around the battle between Ferrari and Matra. In the end the French company emerged triumphant. Its cars proved to be faster and more stable, especially on the faster circuits. The Ferrari 312 Ps won only two victories, at Monza and the Nürburgring, driven on both occasions by Ickx and Redman.

In 1974, Ferrari decided to dedicate its energies only to Formula One, withdrawing after 25 years from the Sports-Prototypes category in which it had obtained such outstanding results.

Technical data

MODEL 312 P
YEAR OF PRODUCTION 1971-1973

ENGINE
position: rear central longitudinal; **cylinders:** 180° 12V-cm³ 2,991 (1973: 2,992); **compression:** 11,5:1; **feed:** Lucas mechanical injection; **ignition:** single; **timing:** 4 valves per cylinder-2 OHC per bank chain driven; **max power:** 324 kW (440 hp) at 10,800 rpm (1973: 338 kW/460 hp at 11,000 rpm).

CHASSIS
gearbox: 5-speed + reverse; **suspensions:** front: wishbones/coil springs — rear: single upper arm, lower wishbones/coil springs; **brakes:** front: discs — rear: discs; **wheelbase** (mm): 2,220 (1973: 2,340).

In the 1971 Sebring 12-Hour, Andretti and Ickx were in the lead with this 312 P, before being forced to retire due to problems with the gearbox.

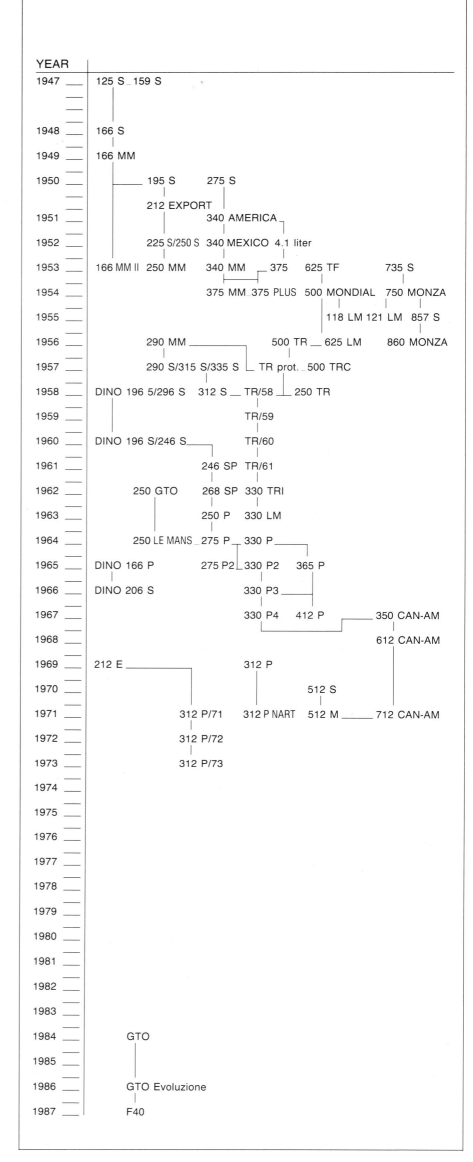

SPORTS-PROTOTYPES

YEAR						
1947	125 S _ 159 S					
1948	166 S					
1949	166 MM					
1950	195 S	275 S				
1951	212 EXPORT	340 AMERICA				
1952	225 S/250 S	340 MEXICO	4.1 liter			
1953	166 MM II	250 MM	340 MM _ 375	625 TF	735 S	
1954	375 MM_375 PLUS	500 MONDIAL	750 MONZA			
1955	118 LM	121 LM	857 S			
1956	290 MM	500 TR _ 625 LM	860 MONZA			
1957	290 S/315 S/335 S	TR prot. 500 TRC				
1958	DINO 196 S/296 S	312 S _ TR/58	250 TR			
1959	TR/59					
1960	DINO 196 S/246 S	TR/60				
1961	246 SP TR/61					
1962	250 GTO	268 SP	330 TRI			
1963	250 P	330 LM				
1964	250 LE MANS _ 275 P	330 P				
1965	DINO 166 P	275 P2	330 P2	365 P		
1966	DINO 206 S	330 P3				
1967	330 P4	412 P	350 CAN-AM			
1968	612 CAN-AM					
1969	212 E	312 P				
1970	512 S					
1971	312 P/71	312 P NART	512 M	712 CAN-AM		
1972	312 P/72					
1973	312 P/73					
1974						
1975						
1976						
1977						
1978						
1979						
1980						
1981						
1982						
1983						
1984	GTO					
1985						
1986	GTO Evoluzione					
1987	F40					

GTO / F40

The GTO Evoluzione constituted a travelling laboratory for testing the solutions that were subsequently to be adopted in the F40.

Created in 1987, in order to celebrate Ferrari's 40th anniversary, this "berlinetta" is conceptually related to the Grand Tourers of the 1950s and 1960s, which managed to score important victories in races, thanks above all to the efforts of a sports-loving clientele. The F40 is technically descended from the GTO of 1984, which gave rise to a series of limited production models in which the Maranello-based company aimed to apply the most advanced construction technology without the limitations imposed by construction on a large scale. The layout of the GTO is based on that of the 308 GTB, but with fundamental modifications such as the longitudinal disposition of the 8-V engine with in-line gearbox and the adoption of an IHI turbocharger for each cylinder bank fitted with an air to air intercooler. Moreover, the 2,855 cm³ engine was provided with a Weber Marelli IAW integrated injection and ignition system and was capable of generating 400 hp at 7,000 rpm, thanks to a supercharged pressure of 0.8 bar. Although the car has never taken part in races, the fact that it can be used either on the road or on the track is proved by its performance, which includes a maximum speed of 187 mph (302 km/h) and acceleration from 0 to 62 mph (0 to 100 km/h) in 4.9 seconds.

The GTO has been followed by an experimental version designated "GTO Evoluzione," which has established a testing ground for particularly sophisticated solutions capable of realizing the sporting potential of the basic model, repeating its general layout, although with a greater emphasis being placed on aerodynamics. In this prototype the engine power is increased to approximately 650 hp at 7,800 rpm, with a maximum speed of almost 217 mph (350 km/h) and an acceleration of 0 to 62 mph (0 to 100 km/h) in 3.6 seconds.

The F40 is thus the direct descendent of this laboratory car. From a structural point of view, the former has a steel tubular space frame with composite elements attached to it. Composite materials have also been used for all the external elements of the bodywork. As far as the aerodynamics are concerned, the lines, designed by Pininfarina, boast a drag co-efficient (Cx) of 0.34 for a resistant surface area of only 0.63 m² despite the remarkable size of the rear wing. The lift co-efficients (Cz) are also remarkably reduced, amouting to 0.04 and 0.15 for the front and rear axles, respectively. The wishbone type suspension has been designed to allow the level of the car's floor from the ground to be regulated in three

positions. An automatic lowering of about 5 in (2 cm) with regard to the standard level occurs at speeds in excess of 75 mph (120 km/h), improving both aerodynamics and stability. Moreover, the driver can also raise the car by the same amount by means of a button. The idea behind this feature is that it facilitates parking maneuvers.

The F40's engine derives directly from that of the GTO, with the main difference lying in an increased supercharged pressure of 1.1 bar. This solution has allowed for a power of 470 hp at 7,000 rpm to be achieved. Some idea of the performance that it is possible to obtain can be gathered from the maximum speed of 201 mph (324 km/h) and an acceleration from 0 to 124 mph (0 to 200 km/h) in just 21.0 seconds.

The 5-speed gearbox (plus reverse) is placed in-line with the engine, and there is a choice between the synchromesh version or that with dog clutches. This is integrated with a limited slip differential. The brake system consists of four ventilated discs with aluminum calipers with four pistons.

The rubber fuel tanks situated on the sides derive from the aeronautical type and are provided with a rapid filler cap like those normally used in endurance races. The sectional wheel rims measure 17 inches in diameter, with 245/40 ZR 17 tires at the front and 335/35 ZR 17 tires to the rear. The spare tire is missing. It has been replaced by a 750 ml aerosol for repairing and blowing up tires.

Technical data

MODEL F40	
YEAR OF PRODUCTION 1987	

ENGINE
position: rear longitudinal; **cylinders:** 90° 8V-cm³ 2,936; **compression:** 7,8:1; **feed:** 2 IHI turbochargers with 2 intercoolers; **ignition:** IAW Weber-Marelli electronic; **timing:** 4 valves per cylinder-2 chain driven OHC per bank; **max power:** 351,5 kW (478 CV) at 7000 rpm; **max torque:** 577 Nm (58,8 kgm) at 4000 rpm.

CHASSIS
gearbox: 5-speed + reverse; **suspensions:** 4 wheel independent, wishbones front and rear, stabilizing bar front and rear; **brakes:** 4 ventilated discs; **steering:** roch-and-tinion; **tires:** front: 245/40 ZR 17 — rear: 335/35 ZR 17.

Ferrari F40

THE FORMULA ONE

The history of the single-seater Ferraris runs parallel to that of the post-war Grand Prix. In fact, the Maranello company has been a protagonist in Formula One races since 1948 (the category was introduced the previous year as "Formula A".)

In the Italian Grand Prix, which took place in Turin in September, three of the first 125 GPs made their debut, with the Frenchman Sommer obtaining a respectable third place. The regulations allowed for 4,500 cm³ aspirated engines or supercharged 1,500 cm³ engines. Enzo Ferrari chose the latter, utilizing the 1,498 cm³ 12-V designed by Gioachino Colombo, providing it with a Roots compressor which raised its power to 225 hp. However, despite a further development carried out in 1949, with the adoption of a two-stage compressor (with 290 hp that increased to 315 hp the following year), Ferrari did not manage to achieve the performance and the results of Alfa Romeo. The latter, with the 158 and 159, eventually generated in the region of 350 hp and won the first two editions of the Driver's World Championship, in 1950 and 1951. In the winter of 1949, the technical management of the Ferrari team was headed by Aurelio Lampredi, who used a new aspirated engine which, in the definitive 4.5-liter version, enabled the 375 F1 to beat its Milanese rivals for the first time in the 1951 British Grand Prix. Nevertheless, this car had a very short lifespan, due to the fact that the following year the World Championship was carried out according to Formula Two regulations, thanks to the lack of contenders caused by Alfa Romeo's withdrawal. This category, which had been introduced in 1948 and forecast the use of 2-liter aspirated engines or 500 cm³ supercharged engines, was the one in which Ferrari had been heavily involved in the 1949-1950 seasons, initially with the 12-cylinder 166 F2 and then with the 500 F2, which used a new 4-cylinder engine. With a displacement of 1,985 cm³, this was capable of generating 170 hp at 7,200 rpm, thanks to sophisticated improvements such as a twincamshaft and dual ignition. The chassis was a tubular spaceframe, with De Dion rear axle. Promoted to Formula One in 1952, the 500 uncontestably dominated the Grand Prix season, allowing Ascari to win the World title, a result which was repeated, with power increased to 180 hp, the following year. In two years, the 500 won 14 Championship races, consisting of 11 victories for Ascari, and one each for Taruffi, Hawthorn, and Farina. In 1954, the Formula One regulations introduced the new limit of 2,500 cm³ for aspirated engines. Faced with this new rule and with only 750 cm³ at their disposal, the supercharged engines stood virtually no chance. In the light of this new formula, Ferrari worked on two different basic designs. On the one hand, it provided the 500 with an engine increased to 2,498 cm³, giving rise to the 625 F1, which had already appeared in 1951 as Free Formula. On the other, it developed the 553 F1 derived from the F2 of the same name of the previous year, provided with a 4-cylinder engine with a displacement that was almost the same as that of the 625, but obtained with a much more oversquared bore/stroke ratio. Both had twin camshaft drive and the feed entrusted to two twin barrel carburetors. The 625 generated 245 hp, and the 553 generated 250 hp.

As far as the chassis was concerned, both these single-seaters had wishbone suspension in the front and a De Dion rear axle with a transverse leaf spring on both axles. The shape of the 553, which caused it to be christened "Shark," was characterized by lateral fuel tanks. The results obtained by the new car were not particularly outstanding, and did not improve with the revised 555 Supershark version of 1955, which could generate 270 hp. In two World Championships dominated by Mercedes, the 625s won two victories: in the 1954 British Grand Prix at Aintree with Gonzales at the wheel, and in the 1955 Monaco Grand Prix with Trintignant at the wheel. The uncertainties regarding the technical management of the team and the superiority of the car team managed by Alfred Neubauer had caused Ferrari to waste much energy on too many fronts, as the umpteenth development to which the 625 was submitted to in 1955 goes to prove. This consisted of the adoption of front coil springs and, like the 555, a 5-speed gearbox.

For the 1956 season, after having received the D50 as a gift from Lancia, Enzo Ferrari also tested an alternative, combining a Supershark chassis with the 8-V engine of the Turin-built car. However, the D50's potential proved to be much greater and it was this car which was entrusted, albeit with several modifications, to Fangio, Collins and Castellotti, with the Argentinian driver winning the title. In 1957, its direct descendent, the 801, was less successful, so much so that preference was given to the development of the new Dino 246 F1. Designed under the direction of Vittorio Jano, this car was derived from the 156 F2 which appeared in the same year. The latter was in practice a smaller version of the 801 from the point of view of its chassis and suspensions. However, its 65° 6-cylinder V engine was entirely new. Dino Ferrari took part in its design before being defeated in a difficult battle against the illness. In its definitive 2,417 cm³ version for Formula One, this engine was capable of generating 270 hp.

In 1958, a new ruling imposed the use of gasoline without additives, which favored the light and maneuverable cars, able to exploit the advantages of lower consumption better. The season centered on the duel between Hawthorn's 246 and Moss' Vanwall. Despite the four victories won by the lat-

ter, it was Ferrari's British driver who took the title in the last race, on the basis of a single outright victory at Reims and a long series of placings. In addition, Collins had won a second victory for Ferrari in the British Grand Prix. At the end of the year, the new champion Hawthorn withdrew from racing, most probably affected by two fatal accidents involving his two teammates Musso and Collins, in France and Germany respectively. Beginning with the Italian Grand Prix, the 246s were fitted with disc brakes, while a new engine increased to 2,474 cm³ and generating 290 hp was developed, destined for the new 256 version. The Dinos were used in Formula One races for another two years. In 1959, they were fitted with elegant bodywork by Fantuzzi, with rear coil spring suspensions. Driven by Brooks and von Trips, they were only narrowly beaten by the rear-engined Cooper-Climaxes, although the British driver won both the French and German Grand Prix. In the following season, the cars' suspensions were further modified, becoming four-wheel independent. The engine was also altered, being slanted in the opposite direction to the previous one. Phil Hill won the only victory of the season at Monza, demonstrating that for Ferrari too the time had come to adopt the rear-engine for the new 1,500 cm³ Formula One that was to be used in 1961. In fact, the new 156 F1 won the world title for the American Phil Hill, obtaining other satisfactory results untill 1964; the same year Lorenzo Bandini won the Austrian Grand Prix, the last glorious victory for a Ferrari 6-cylinder single-seater.

In that year, the Maranello company's strongest car was the new 158 F1, which permitted John Surtees to take the World Championship title thanks to two victories obtained at the Nürburgring and Monza, as well as a series of placings. The Championship was decided by the last race in the program, the Mexican Grand Prix, in which Surtees, Clark and G. Hill all had practically the same chance of winning the final victory. However, the Ferrari driver gained the upper hand, thanks above all to Bandini's help. After having slowed down Hill, on the last lap he gave his determining second place to his teammate. In the last two races of the 1964 season, in the United States and Mexico, the Ferrari cars were entered with the blue and white colors of NART as a form of protest against the Italian Sports Commission, which Enzo Ferrari felt had done nothing to prevent the new 250 Le Mans from not being granted international homologation in the GT category.

The 158 adopted the same semi-monocoque chassis that had been introduced on the 156 toward the end of the 1963 season. The engine was a 90° 8-cylinder V with a capacity of 1,489 cm³, characterized by Bosch direct injection and dual ignition, generating approximately 210 hp. It had twin camshafts with two valves per cylinder. At the same time, Ferrari had continued to develop the new 180° 12-cylinder V designed by Mauro Forghieri and driven during its debut by Bandini in the 1964 United States Grand Prix, on a chassis similar to that of the 158. The car on which it was mounted was christened 1512 F1, and with a displacement of 1,498 cm³, in the single ignition version, it could generate 220 hp, thanks to the new Lucas injection system. In 1965, the power increased to 225 hp, due to the adoption of two spark plugs per cylinder. However, Ferrari, which had used both the 158 and the 1512 in that year, did not obtain any victories in what was to be the last season for the 1.5-liter single-seaters, which were to be forced into retirement by the new 3,000 cm³ limit of 1966. Ferrari wasted no time in entering the 312, which however lasted for four not particularly successful seasons. Afterwards, appeared the new single-seaters provided with the new 12-cylinder boxer engines. The first of these was the 312 B, introduced in 1970 and driven by Jacky Ickx, joined, according to the occasion, either by Ignazio Giunti or Clay Regazzoni. The 2,991 cm³ (2,992 cm³ from 1972), probably Forghieri's masterpiece, was capable of generating 455 hp at 11,500 rpm which, at the end of a successful 10-year career, had gradually increased to 515 hp at 12,300 rpm. The twin camshafts with four valves per cylinder, the Lucas injection, and the Dinoplex electronic ignition were features which remained unaltered throughout this period. The innovations that were gradually carried out on the chassis were much more significant. The 312 B was rather a conventional car, with the typical Ferrari semi-monocoque which was lengthened on the rear top to support the engine.

The suspensions also followed the classical nature of the front axle with upper rocker arm and lower wishbone with "inboard" dampers, and rear suspension with a single upper arm, lower wishbone, two trailing radius rods, and external dampers. Satisfactory results were obtained, with a competitiveness that lasted throughout 1970, embodied by Ickx's three victories in Austria, Canada, and Mexico, and that of Regazzoni in Italy. To these was added the first place obtained by Mario Andretti in the first race of the following season in South Africa, after which the 312 B was perhaps replaced too quickly by the 312 B2. This was very similar in general layout, but with new rear suspension consisting of an upper wishbone acting on the internal spring-damper units mounted in a horizontal position. The brakes on the rear axle were also linked to the differential exit.

Despite Ickx's victory in the Netherlands in wet conditions, the car did not find its optimum form, allowing the Tyrrell driven by Stewart to dominate the Championship. Things did not improve in 1973, with the 312 B3, developed by Colombo and provided with a monocoque chassis (with side coolers) built in England by John Thompson. Entirely ineffective, the B3 was placed in the hands of Forghieri who, toward the end of the season, made it into a valid base for the new single-seater of the same name which appeared the following year. This car marked the beginning of the successful partnership between the Ferrari and Niki Lauda, who twice won the World Championship in 1975 and 1977. The Austrian driver dominated the 1975 season at the wheel of his 312 T with transverse gearbox. The following year, thanks to a series of victories obtained in the early part of the season (in Brazil and South Africa with the same car, and then in Belgium, Monaco, and Great Britain with the revised 312 T2), Lauda was heading for an easy conquest of the title for the second time when the tragic accident at the Nürburgring caused him to miss the next two Grand Prix. With great courage, he returned to racing at Monza, losing the title in the last race in Japan, where he chose to retire due to the terrible weather conditions. In the same year, Regazzoni gained a victory at Long Beach. Lauda only had to wait until 1977 to vindicate himself. Still at the wheel of the T2, he once again took the world title thanks to the three victories won in South Africa, Germany, and the Netherlands and no fewer than six second places. Carlos Reutemann, his new teammate, won the Brazilian Grand Prix. Lauda withdrew from the team after the United States Grand Prix had guaranteed him the title. In the two remaining races of the season, he was replaced by Gilles Villeneuve. This demonstrated great intuition on the part of Enzo Ferrari, who wanted him in the team although Villeneuve had only shown vague signs of promise at the time. In 1978, Reutemann won the Brazilian Grand Prix, once again with the T2, before the debut of the new 312 T3 took place in South Africa. This new single-seater had been designed above all for the Michelin radial tires which Ferrari had adopted instead of the traditional cross ply Goodyear tires. The Argentinian driver took first place at Long Beach, Brands Hatch, and Watkins Glen, while in his native country, Villeneuve won the last race of the season. It was in this contest that Mario Andretti took the Championship title with the ''ground effect'' Lotus that led all manufacturers to follow the same path. With this aim, Ferrari studied the 312 T4 for the 1979 season, entrusting it to Jody Scheckter and Villeneuve. Due to the width of the 12-cylinder boxer engine, the aerodynamics of the underside of the new car — characterized by wide flanks with sliding miniskirts — did not achieve the effectiveness of the single-seaters fitted with the less powerful but narrower Cosworth 8-V. Nevertheless, the T4 proved to be extremely competitive, allowing the South African driver to win the World Championship title with victories in the Belgian, Montecarlo and Italian Grand Prix, as well as three second places and numerous placings in point-earning positions. Villeneuve was relegated to second place in the final classification despite an identical number of victories (obtained at Kyalami, Long Beach and Watkins Glen) and four second places. In 1980, the same two drivers had the new 312 T5 at their disposal, designed to improve the ground effect. With this aim, in depth studies were carried out in the Pininfarina wind tunnel, while the engine was fitted with new heads that reduced its width by about two inches (5 cm). The extremely rapid aerodynamic progress of the cars with Cosworth engines nevertheless annulled the efforts of Ferrari, which obtained only sporadic placings. In order to return to the top, the Maranello company therefore made a precise choice: the turbocharged engine. The supercharged era had characterized single-seaters for a decade, from 1981 until 1988 when this type was no longer permitted by the regulations. Initially forced to submit to this turn-about in the rules by several British manufacturers who needed to provide further life sap for their aspirated engine cars, in 1982, the Ferrari turbos experienced a simultaneous exalting and tragic moment. The great successes scored by Villeneuve and Pironi, enabled them to take the Championship title in that year with their 126 C2. At the same time, the Canadian driver lost his life in the Belgian Grand Prix, while following a serious accident at Hockenheim, the Frenchman was forced to withdraw from the race.

Ferrari came close to taking the title once again in 1985, with Michele Alboreto at the wheel of the F1/85 but he was beaten in the second half of the season by Prost's McLaren. Ferrari was thus subjected to the predominance of the Honda engine single-seaters, a superiority that was broken only toward the end of the 1987 season by the F1/87 driven by Gerhard Berger who won the Grand Prix in Japan itself and, immediately after, the Australian Grand Prix.

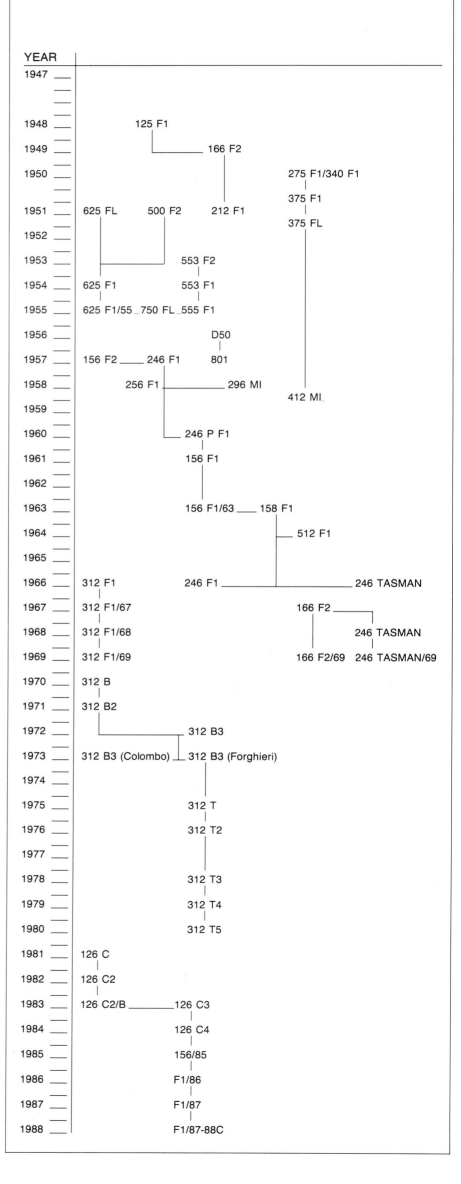

375 F1

In 1951, with the 375 F1 fitted with a 4.5-liter 12-cylinder aspirated engine, Enzo Ferrari was able to gain his first Grand Prix victory, achieving his aim of beating the 1.5-liter supercharged Alfa Romeos, against which the earlier 125 F1 with supercharger had been powerless. The development program of the 375 was launched in 1950, and was undertaken by 31 year-old Aurelio Lampredi, who had arrived at the company the previous winter. Behind the choice of an aspirated engine lay the consideration that, despite the fact that it had a slightly smaller power than a supercharger, it consumed far less, and this would permit it to cover the distances called for in a Grand Prix, generally 310 miles (500 km) at that time. The Alfettas covered this distance burning up some 100 U.S. gals (400 liters) of alcohol mixture, making one less refuelling stop.

Lampredi wanted a light and simple engine. This resulted in the adoption of a single overhead camshaft and cast iron cylinder liners screwed to the heads which, like the crankcase, were built in light alloy. However, the basic layout remained typical of Ferrari, with 12-cylinder arranged in a 60° V, fed by three carburetors with dry sump lubrication. The displacement was originally 3,322 cm³ in the 275 F1, which made its debut in the Belgian Grand Prix in June. However, in the course of the season it increased initially to 4,102 cm³ (340 F1) with an increase in bore, and finally to 4,494 cm³, thanks to an increase in stroke. It had a 4-speed gearbox. The chassis, consisting of a tubular ladder frame, was also subject to careful design, aimed at obtaining maximum maneuverability, which proved to be remarkable thanks to the De Dion rear axle with lower transverse leaf springs. The disc brakes were hydraulically controlled with two cylinders per wheel.

The 375 F1 made its debut toward the end of the 1950 season, and it obtained its first victory in the non-Championship Spanish Grand Prix, with Ascari at the wheel. The new 4.5-liter was not used in World Championship competition until the final race at Monza, in which two took part, one driven by Ascari and the other by Dorino Serafini. After having completed 15 laps of the race, Ascari's rear axle broke out, driving his teammate's car, he managed to finish in second place. The car used by the two Italian drivers was subsequently acquired by an Englishman, Tony Vanderwell. He drove it in 1952, with several modifications, under the name of Thin Wall Special. With a compression ratio of 11:1, the 375 had a power of 350 hp at 7,000 rpm, increased to 360 hp at 7,300 rpm at the beginning of the 1951 season.

The same year, Lampredi prepared a version with dual ignition, capable of generating 380 hp at 7,500 rpm, with a compression ratio of 12:1. The car's competitiveness gradually increased until the "historic" British Grand Prix which took place on the Silverstone circuit on July 14: Ferrari succeeded in winning a World Championship race for the first time, with Gonzales at the wheel of a single ignition 375. The Argentinian driver finished the race with an average of just under 96 mph (155 km/h), some 51 seconds ahead of the Alfa Romeo 159 driven by Fangio, following a captivating duel lasting two hours and 45 minutes. The remainder of the season saw two further successes scored by the Maranello-built 4.5 liters: one at the Nürburgring and another at Monza driven by Ascari. These three victories in seven races demonstrated an increasing superiority on the part of the Modenese company over Alfa, which realized that the life cycle of its own supercharged cars had come to an end, although Fangio succeeded in winning the title. Thus the Milanese company decided to withdraw from racing, an event which was indirectly responsible for the premature exit of the 375 from the scene. In fact, the regulations which allowed aspirated engines with superchargers of 4.5 liters and 1.5 liters, respectively should have remained in practice until 1953, but due to the lack of competitors expected for the 1952 season, the C.S.I. decided to limit the World Championship to Formula Two.

The final evolution of the 375 was the version which Ferrari intended to enter in the Indianapolis 500-Mile race that year. This single-seater had a power of 400 hp at 7,500 rpm and a front axle with coil springs. Qualifying in 19th place on the American circuit at over 134 mph (216 km/h), Ascari was forced to retire during the race due to the breakage of a wheel hub.

Technical data

MODEL 375 F1
YEAR OF PRODUCTION 1951

ENGINE
position: front longitudinal; **cylinders:** 60° 12V-cm³ 4,494; **compression:** 12,0:1; **feed:** 3 Weber 46DCF3 carburetors; **ignition:** dual; **timing:** 2 valves per cylinder-1 OHC per bank chain driven; **max power:** 282 kW (384 hp) at 7,500 rpm.

CHASSIS
gearbox: 4-speed + reverse; **suspensions:** front: wishbones/transverse leaf springs — rear: De Dion axle/transverse leaf springs; **brakes:** front: drums — rear: drums; **wheelbase** (mm): 2,320.

Ferrari's first victory in a world Grand Prix was won at Silverstone in 1951, with a 375 F1 driven by Froilan Gonzales.

Ferrari 375 F1

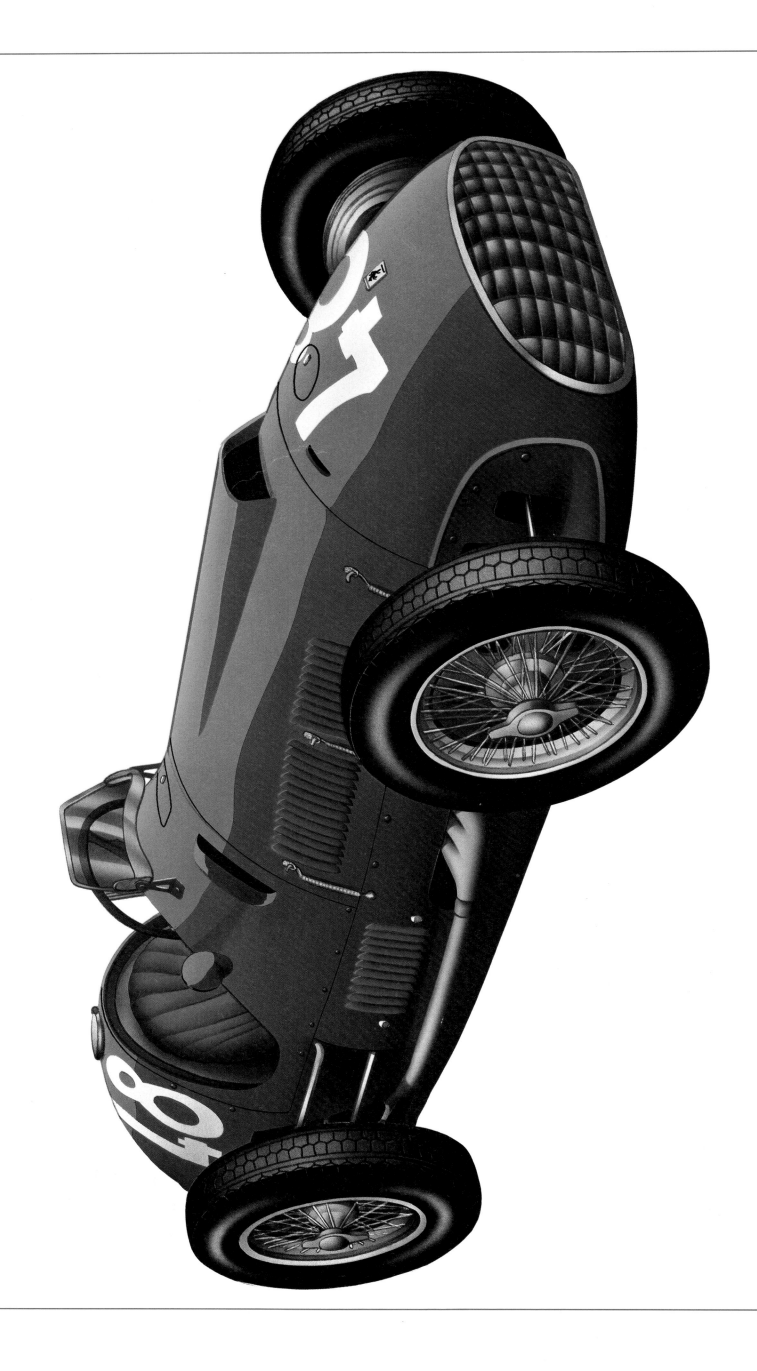

Lancia-Ferrari D50

Lancia-Ferrari D50 / 801

Hawthorn (n. 8) and Collins (n. 7) lead during the initial phase of the 1957 German Grand Prix at the wheel of their 801s.

The Ferrari D50 was a car that led a double life. In fact, it was born bearing the Lancia insignia in 1954, the year in which it was only entered in the last Grand Prix in Spain, driven by Alberto Ascari, who had obtained a pole-position in trials but was forced to withdraw during the race due to troubles with the clutch. In the 1955 season, the last of the "Mercedes era" following a Grand Prix in Argentina that was not particularly successful, Lancia obtained good results at Montecarlo, with Castellotti coming in second place. This occurred after Ascari, who had been in the lead, had driven into the sea without any serious consequences. However on May 26, the driver from Lodi died in an accident at Monza at the wheel of a Ferrari Sport. This lead the Turin-based company to announce its withdrawal from racing. However, in the next Grand Prix in Germany, Castellotti persuaded Lancia to enter a car with which he obtained the best qualifying time.

In fact, the burden of running an F.1 team had proved to be particularly heavy for Lancia at a time in which the company had financial problems which were subsequently to lead to the Carlo Pesenti group takeover in 1956. Gianni Lancia, who did not wish to disperse a valuable technical patrimony, gave all his single-seaters to Ferrari, in an agreement which also involved Fiat, that guaranteed the Maranello company considerable financing for five years. Three D50s, bearing prancing horse on their sides, reappeared on the Monza track in trials carried out by Farina, Villoresi, and Castellotti. These, however, were not used in the race itself due to the unreliability of the Englebert tires that they were forced contractually to adopt. Together with the D50s, their designer Vittorio Jano also arrived at Maranello. The conception of these cars was very different from that in vogue for F1 at the time. Very light and compact, this car that was subsequently to be unofficially christened Lancia-Ferrari possessed an unusual weight distribution, with the external fuel tanks on the bodywork occupying practically the entire space between the front and rear wheels. This change allowed for an enormous reduction in the variations of the height of the car's floor due to the gradual consumption of the more than 53 U.S.gals (200 liters) of mixed blend needed to cover the 310 miles (500 km) of the Grand Prix at the time.

Moreover, its normal behavior when taking a corner was the result of the concentration of the masses inside the wheelbase. Despite the fact that this allowed for very high cornering limits, there was little warning when these limits were reached, something that did not appeal to the drivers. The front suspension consisted of equal-length tubular wishbones, lower transverse leaf springs and "in-board" telescopic dampers. In the rear there was a De Dion axle with lower transverse leaf springs and hydraulic

dampers. The transmission was the "transaxle" type with transverse gearbox in block with a rear differential.

The drum brakes were hydraulic. The light alloy engine, with cast iron wet cylinder liners, was a 90° 8-V of 2,488 cm^3 and almost perfectly square, with twin camshaft timing and a feed with four twin barrel carburetors, and power of 250 hp at 8,100 rpm. It was mounted in an oblique position, thus making it possible for the driveshaft to pass to the left of the driving seat. The driving seats, in turn, was much lower creating an advantage for the entire front section of the car. During the winter of 1954-55, Ferrari carried out important modifications on the original project. First, with the aim of improving the car's handling, the mass was moved to the rear with the adoption of a main tank in the tail. The sides were incorporated into the bodywork, and the exhaust pipes were placed inside them. Previously, these had run along the bottom of the car. The official team for the 1956 season included Fangio, Collins, and Castellotti, who were joined on various occasions by Musso, Gendebien, Frère, Pilette, and De Portago. Fangio won the world title thanks to his victories on the Buenos Aires, Silverstone, and Nürburgring tracks, and a second place at Monza, gained through the generosity of Collins, who handed his own car over to him. For his part, the British driver won the Belgian and French Grand Prix. During the winter break, the D50s were completely overhauled to make way for the new 801. The engine was rendered more oversquared with modifications in the size of the bore and stroke (which had already been altered half-way through the 1956 season) leading to a slight increase in the engine capacity to 2,495 cm^3, with a power of 275 hp at 7,500 rpm. Moreover, the suspensions adopted coil springs instead of leaf springs, while the original lateral fuel tanks disappeared entirely. The whole car was much heavier due to the adoption of a chassis with larger section tubes.

Collins, Musso, and Hawthorn, joined on occasions by Castellotti, Gonzales, Perdisa, Trintignant, and von Trips, never succeeded in achieving more than a good finishing position throughout the 1957 season, and at the end of the season the 801 was abandoned to make way for the new 6-cylinder Dinos.

In 1956, the Lancia-Ferrari D50 won three Grand Prix with Juan Manuel Fangio at the wheel and two driven by Peter Collins.

Technical data

MODEL LANCIA-FERRARI D50
YEAR OF PRODUCTION 1955-1956

ENGINE
position: front longitudinal; **cylinders:** 90° 8V-cm^3 2,488; **compression:** 9,2:1; **feed:** 4 Solex 40PII carburetors; **ignition:** dual; **timing:** 2 valves per cylinder-2 OHC per bank chain driven; **max power:** 184 kW (250 hp) at 8,100 rpm.

CHASSIS
gearbox: 5-speed + reverse; **suspensions:** front: wishbones/transverse leaf spring — rear: De Dion axle/transverse leaf spring; **brakes:** front: drums — rear: drums; **wheelbase** (mm): 2,280.

156 F1

The first rear-engine single-seater Ferrari was the experimental 246 F1 of 1960.

Surtees won the 1963 German Grand Prix at the wheel of a Ferrari 156.

The change in regulations that introduced 1,500 cm³ engines into Formula One racing in 1961, allowed the Maranello company to exploit its experience acquired with the 65° 6-cylinder V engine designed with this displacement by Vittorio Jano in 1957 and subsequently increased to 2.4 liters for use on the 246 F1. Twice during the 1960 season, in World Championship Grand Prix races, Ferrari had entered a single-seater with rear engine: the experimental 2.4 liters 246 P at Munich, and the same car in a 1.5 liters version developed for Formula Two at Monza. An avid supporter of the engine placed directly behind the driver was Carlo Chiti, Ferrari's technical director at the time, who campaigned for the adoption of this solution, despite resistance from the managerial staff of the company itself. Thus Chiti became the artificer of the project for the new 156, for which he studied a variant of Jano's 6V engine with a 120° angle between the cylinder banks instead of 65°, and a lighter weight of only 265 lb (102 kg), due to the fact that almost all of the components were made of light alloy. The bore and stroke retained the same values as the 1960 Formula Two engine, with a displacement of 1,477 cm³, just as the timing was chain driven twin camshaft. The ignition system had two spark plugs per cylinder, while the engine feed was entrusted to two triple barrel carburetors. The new engine had a power of 190 hp at 9,500 rpm, while that of the 65° version, whose displacement was increased to 1,481 cm³, had one of 185 hp at the same number of rpm.

The extremely simple tubular space frame was conceived so that it could also house the 65° V version, with the aim of exploiting the existing engines and using them in a greater number of cars. The 120° version also had the advantage of weighing 44 lb (20 kg) less. Both had five speed gearboxes.

The suspensions followed the classic pattern for single-seaters at the time: both axles had double wishbones with sets of springs and dampers on the wheels. The narrow and tapered bodywork was characterized by the typical arrow-shaped nose with double air inlets. The 156, still at an experimental stage, made its debut on April 25, 1961, in the non-Championship Syracuse Grand Prix, which ended in a victory for Giancarlo Baghetti. The first car with 120° engine was entrusted to Ginther at Montecarlo, in the opening race for the World Championship. Apart from Ginther, who served as a test driver, the official Ferrari cars were driven in the course of the season by Wolfgang von Trips and Phil Hill. Starting with the Belgian Grand Prix, a fourth single-seater with 65° engine was entered, being driven on various occasions by Gendebien, Baghetti, and Mairesse. At Monza there was even a fifth 156 driven by Ricardo Rodriguez. Von Trips took first place in the

Netherlands and England, Baghetti in France and Phil Hill in Belgium and Italy. Phil Hill won the world title at Monza, on a day that was clouded by the accident which killed von Trips and 14 spectators. Ferrari withdrew from the last race in the United States before a winter in which the team was plagued by internal problems that led to the resignation of men such as Chiti, Bizzarrini, and another six managers. As well as a project for a 24-valve 156 engine and a design for an air-cooled transverse 8-V that were never followed up, the former staff had left a new gearbox located in the center between the engine and the differential. This configuration, which gave rise to the so-called 156 short tail, was used in 1962 solely at Montecarlo. Ferrari preferred to adopt the old outboard gearbox in the other races. The technical management was taken over by Rocchi and Salvarani, aided by Bazzi, Jano, Bellei, and Forghieri, who soon assumed the role of leader of the group.

The next season, with the same team of drivers as well as Lorenzo Bandini on occasions, proved to be a lean one. In fact, all the World Championship races were dominated by the new British 8-cylinder single-seaters. In the German Grand Prix a substantially modified version of the 156 appeared, with a similar but lighter space frame, modified suspensions, wider tracks, nose provided with traditional air inlet, light alloy wheels, and a new 6-speed gearbox. Further innovations were introduced in 1963, with the adoption of a semi-monocoque chassis and rear suspension that utilized the new pattern with front upper rocker arms and rear double radius rods. As far as the 120° engine was concerned, a Bosch direct injection system was employed, allowing for an increase in power to 205 hp at 10,500 rpm.

Mairesse was initially called to back up John Surtees, the new chief driver, and was followed by Ludovico Scarfiotti and then Lorenzo Bandini. Surtees won a good second place in England and an outright victory at the Nürburgring.

Technical data

MODEL 156 F1	
YEAR OF PRODUCTION 1961-1963	

ENGINE
position: rear central longitudinal; **cylinders:** 120° 6V-cm³ 1,477; **compression:** 9,8:1; **feed:** 2 Weber 40IF3C carburetors; **ignition:** dual; **timing:** 2 valves per cylinder-2 OHC per bank chain driven; **max power:** 140 kW (190 hp) at 9,500 rpm.

CHASSIS
gearbox: 5-speed + reverse; **suspensions:** front: wishbones/coil springs — rear: wishbones/coil springs; **brakes:** front: discs — rear: discs; **wheelbase** (mm): 2,300.

Ferrari 156 F1

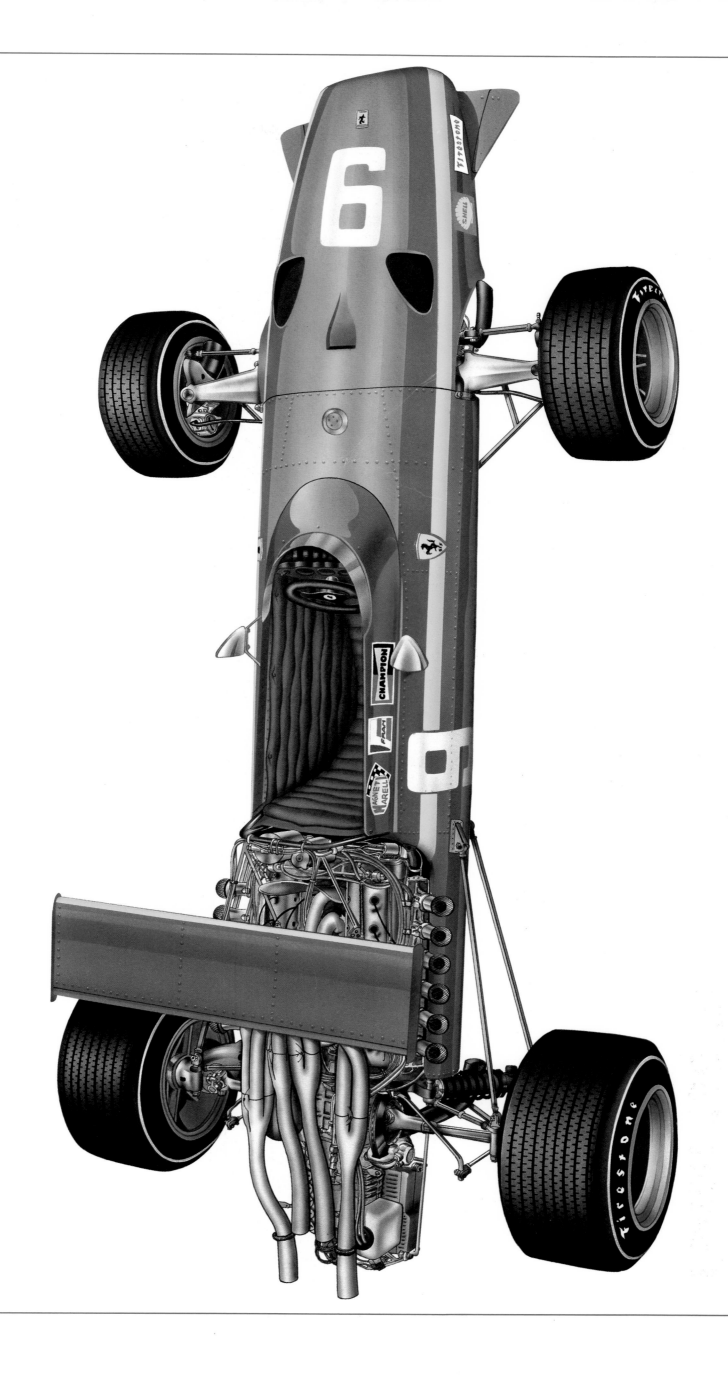

Ferrari 312 F1/1968

312 F1

The 1969 version of the 312 F1 was characterized by lateral exhausts.

For the new 3,000 cm³ Formula One that entered the racing world in 1966, Ferrari could boast an advantage over its British rivals since it already had an available valid engine: the "short" 3-liter 60° 12-V descended from one designed by Colombo. In practice, this engine underwent heavy development for the occasion. In fact, although it retained the 77 mm bore of almost all earlier 275 and 330 versions, a particularly short stroke was adopted, bringing the engine capacity to 2,989 cm³. The feed possessed a Lucas injection system, while the Dinoplex electronic ignition activated two spark plugs per cylinder. There was twin camshaft timing, producing 360 hp at 10,000 rpm. The exhaust manifolds were located on the exterior of the V formed by the cylinders.

The chassis was not unlike the semi-monocoque frames of the earlier 158 and 512 F1. The forward suspensions employed an upper rocker arm and a lower wishbone with internal coil springs and dampers. In the rear, there was a single upper arm and a lower wishbone, integrated by two parallel trailing radius rods.

The car's racing debut resulted in a victory for Surtees at the non-Championship Syracuse Grand Prix in 1966. Its first success in World Championship racing occurred in the Belgian Grand Prix, in which Surtees was first over the finish line (a few days before he left the team). After a second place gained by Parkes at Reims, the new Ferrari, driven by Parkes and Bandini, did not succeed in beating its rivals (especially Brabham-Repco). This situation continued until the Italian Grand Prix, in which the Maranello company entered three 3-liter single-seaters.

For the Monza race, the power of the engine was increased to 375 hp thanks to the adoption of new heads with three valves per cylinder. Scarfiotti won the race, with his teammate Parkes gaining second place. Ferrari's last race of the season was the following U.S. Grand Prix, from which the only 312, driven by Bandini, was forced to withdraw. The "36 valve" engine had a slight

innovation in the 1967 season. The exhaust pipes this time were placed between the two cylinder banks. Moreover, its power was slightly increased to 385 hp, again obtained at 10,000 rpm.

For the bodywork, elements in glass fiber and aluminum resulted in a weight reduction, compared to the first 312 F1, of 88 lb (40 kg). After having withdrawn from the first Grand Prix event of the season in South Africa, Ferrari experienced a tragic day at Montecarlo, clouded by Lorenzo Bandini's fatal accident. Amon took third place on the Montecarlo circuit, a result which the New Zealand driver repeated in Belgium, England, and Germany. This difficult period was also marked by Parkes' serious accident a Spa and Scarfiotti's withdrawal from the team. At Monza, as in the previous year, Ferrari further developed its 12-cylinder engine, which was provided with four valves and a single spark plug per cylinder. This resulted in a power of 390 hp at 10,500 rpm. With a team consisting of Amon, Ickx and De Adamich (De Adamich only participated in the initial race at Kyalami), Ferrari did not obtain outstanding results in the 1968 season. Starting with the Belgian Grand Prix, the Ferrari 312 F1 was fitted with a rear airfoil installed over the engine. The latter now generated 405 hp at 11,000 rpm. The Ferrari team obtained the best results with Jacky Ickx, who won the French Grand Prix as well as a series of good placings. Chris Amon earned points in only three of the twelve races. He did take second place at Rouen behind his own teammate. Toward the end of the year, several modifications carried out on the engine resulted in an increased power of 412 hp at 10,500 rpm. For the new season, the engine, once again in the "48-valve" version, was further updated. The air inlet pipes were placed once again between the cylinder banks, while the exhaust pipes were once more situated outside of the latter. The power increased to 436 hp at 11,000 rpm.

1969 was characterized by regulation problems concerning the use of the rear airfoils. Initially it was abolished by the C.S.I. on the eve of the Monaco Grand Prix then starting with the Dutch Grand Prix, it was reinstated, but with size limits that were more in accordance with safety needs. In this context, the 312 F1, initially possessing a hydraulically adjustable wing, was eventually equipped with rear aerodynamic appendages in several original shapes. With only one car driven by Chris Amon (joined on rare occasions by a second car driven by Pedro Rodriguez), Ferrari did not obtain any important results, although proved to be sufficiently fast on all tracks. The only points obtained by Amon valid for the World Championship were the four gained by his third place at Zandvoort.

The 312 F1 was not one of the most successful of Ferrari's racing cars. However, one must keep in mind that it had to withstand the appearance of the Ford-Cosworth engine during its career. Nevertheless it was one of the most enduring Maranello single-seaters, and the last to be fitted with a 12-cylinder V engine before the introduction of the new boxer type.

Technical data

MODEL 312 F1
YEAR OF PRODUCTION 1968

ENGINE
position: rear central longitudinal; **cylinders:** 60° 12V-cm³ 2,989; **compression:** 9,2:1; **feed:** Lucas mechanical injection; **ignition:** dual; **timing:** 4 valves per cylinder-2 OHC per bank chain driven; **max power:** 298 kW (405 hp) at 11,000 rpm.

CHASSIS
gearbox: 5-speed + reverse; **suspensions:** front: upper rocker arms, lower wishbones/coil springs — rear: single upper arms, lower wishbones/coil springs; **brakes:** front: discs — rear: discs; **wheelbase** (mm): 2,400.

312 T

In 1975, with the 312 T, Ferrari was able to reconquer the World Championship title. Presented in September 1974, this single-seater was designed by Mauro Forghieri on the basis of the technology typical of the Maranello-built Formula One cars at the time. This included the monocoque chassis that had been constructed by riveting aluminum panels to a framework of square tubes, reinforced internally by steel and synthetic elements.

The compactness of the whole was remarkable, with all the principal masses being concentrated in the wheelbase-track area. An important contribution to this effect was the adoption of a new transverse gearbox (hence the abbreviated initial T) combined with the 2,991.8 cm³ 12-cylinder boxer engine (fitted with Lucas injection and Dinoplex Marelli electronic ignition) that had become remarkably reliable, despite achieving a range of 490-500 hp at 12,200 rpm. The 312's origins can be traced to the decisive change of technical direction introduced by Ferrari in 1970 with the 312 B3. Following a practice that British manufacturers had employed for many years, this car, for the first time, used a monocoque frame. The car was designed by Sandro Colombo, who had been entrusted with the team's technical direction in Forghieri's place. However, the vehicle proved to be too heavy and not sufficiently competitive, so Forghieri was once again entrusted with carrying out the necessary modifications (which appeared at the Austrian Grand Prix). The car showed immediate improvement, and as a result, the following year a new version was prepared. It was once again designated B3 and had an advanced cockpit and new suspensions. In 1974, Regazzoni lost a world title that seemed to be practically conquered in the final race, while his teammate Niki Lauda proved his great potential, winning two victories in Spain and the Netherlands, as compared

to the Swiss driver's only victory, scored at the Nürburgring. The 312 T retained the best of the B3/74, with further improvements being made to the aerodynamics and the suspensions. As far as the latter were concerned, the front suspension utilized an original system with upper rocker arms worked by internal groups of springs and dampers inclined at 50°. It was attached below to a small flange which also acted as a support for the anti-roll bar and one of the lower wishbone arms. In the rear, the brakes were no longer situated "in-board", but on the wheels. In addition, there was a single upper radius rods and lower reversed wishbones.

The fuel tanks, which had a maximum capacity of 50 U.S. gals (190 liters), were located on the cockpit's sides. The water and oil coolers were situated in front of the rear wheels and behind

The 312 T made one of its first appearances in a series of tests out at Vallelunga in February 1985.

In 1976, before his accident at the Nürburgring, Niki Lauda took second place at Jarama and first place at Zolder, Montecarlo and Brands Hatch with the 312 T2.

Ferrari 312 T

The cockpit of the 312 T2 of 1976, the year in which Ferrari won the Manufacturer's Championship.

the front wheels, respectively. The 1975 season, in which the 312 T was driven by Niki Lauda and Clay Regazzoni, proved to be a triumphant one. Following a quiet debut in the South African Grand Prix, the Austrian driver gained victories at Montecarlo, Zolder, Anderstorp, Le Castellet, and Watkins Glen, as well as a successful result in the non-Championship "Daily Express Trophy" at Silverstone.

Lauda won the World Championship title, while his teammate, who occupied the highest step on the podium at Monza as well as at a non-Championship race in Dijon, took fifth place in the overall classification. The 312 T continued also to win in the following season, in which it was used until the 312 T2 made its debut. The latter constituted a direct evolution. It was modified above all in view of the new regulations which abolished the large "periscope" air inlets behind the cockpit and imposed a roll-bar in the front part of the cockpit too. In 1976, Lauda won the Brazilian and South African Grand Prix with the 312 T, while Regazzoni was first at Long Beach. Five 312 Ts were built, winning a total of 11 victories in no less than 19 races, a result obtained by few other cars in the history of automobile racing.

Technical data

MODEL 312 T
YEAR OF PRODUCTION 1975

ENGINE
position: rear central longitudinal; **cylinders:** 180° 12V-cm³ 2,992; **compression:** 11,5:1; **feed:** Lucas mechanical injection; **ignition:** single; **timing:** 4 valves per cylinder-2 OHC per bank chain driven; **max power:** 360 kW (490 hp) at 12,200 rpm.

CHASSIS
gearbox: 5-speed + reverse; **suspensions:** front: upper rocker arms, lower wishbones/coil springs — rear: upper radius rods, lower wishbones/coil springs; **brakes:** front: discs — rear: discs; **wheelbase** (mm): 2,518.

The rear axle of the Ferrari 312 T consisted of an inverted lower trailing arm and an upper transverse arm, an example both of simplicity and efficiency.

126 C-C2-C3

Following the example of Renault which, from 1977, had courageously chosen the path of supercharging for its Formula One engines, Ferrari presented its first one-seater "turbo" in June, 1980. The new 126 C made its track debut during the Italian Grand Prix that took place at Imola in September, although it was not used in competition until the next season. The project was the work of Mauro Forghieri and his staff of Rocchi, Salvarani, and Marchetti.

The new engine, which was a 120° 6-cylinder V, had a displacement of 1,496 cm^3 and its intake was situated on the exterior of the cylinder banks, while the exhaust was high up. The engine feed was provided by two KKK turbocompressors and a Lucas mechanical injection system. The timing was twin camshaft with four valves per cylinder, generating 540 hp at 11,000 rpm. In the winter of 1980-81, in depth research had also been carried out on supercharging by means of Comprex, but considering the advantages of the turbo in terms of power and consumption, this had been abandoned. Combined with the engine there was also a 5-speed transverse gearbox. This extremely advanced engine was paired with a rather conventional chassis, which had the semi-monocoque structure typical of Ferrari. As far as the suspensions were concerned, both axles had a single upper rocker arm with lower wishbones and in board-mounted spring-damper units.

The car's racing debut took place in the 1981 Argentinian Grand Prix, driven by Gilles Villeneuve and Didier Pironi, both of whom were forced to retire. Nevertheless, the 126 C made rapid progress, so much so that the Maranello company's two drivers led for a long time in the San Marino Grand Prix, and, following a fourth place in Belgium, the Canadian gained an excellent victory at Montecarlo, followed immediately after by one on the Spanish circuit of Jarama. At the end of the season, although the new Ferrari had not achieved sensational results, it had proved the effectiveness of the turbo engine, while revealing inadequacies as far as the chassis and aerodynamics were concerned.

Harvey Postlethwaite was called upon to design a new car, and he created Ferrari's first true monocoque (without counting the unsuccessful B3 of 1973). It consisted of two superimposed semi-shells in aluminum honeycomb panels with reinforcements in carbon fiber. The suspensions were also updated, and starting with the Canadian Grand Prix a new form was adopted in the front with twin swinging wishbones and transverse pullrod. This solution was introduced by Brabham in 1981, and merged efficiency with the clarity of the aerodynamic flow that lapped its sides.

The engine, which had revised cooling ducts and the covers of the tappets painted red, was provided with the new "Emul-system" in which the mixture entering the cylinders was emulsioned using a small quantity of water with the aim of reducing the combustion temperature. This solution made it possible to increase the supercharging pressure, generating 580 hp at 11,000 rpm.

The 1982 season thus began in a promising fashion for the new 126 C2s, which took third place at Long Beach with Villeneuve at the wheel (he was subsequently disqualified for irregularities regarding the spoiler) and the first two places at Imola, with Pironi being followed by the Canadian. However, the next Grand Prix in Belgium had a negative effect on the whole season, caused by the fatal trial accident which deprived the world of Formula One racing of one of the best-loved drivers in its entire history: Gilles Villeneuve. Pironi then took second place at Montecarlo and Brands Hatch, third place at Detroit and in France, and, lastly, an outright victory in the Netherlands, mortgaging the world title. However, another adverse event prevented the French driver from becoming World Champion, namely a serious accident at Hockenheim that forced him to withdraw from racing. The German Grand Prix was won, however, by Patrik Tambay, who had

In 1981, Gilles Villeneuve obtained two consecutive victories at Montecarlo and Jarama at the wheel of his 126 C.

been called in to drive the second Ferrari car. The final result of the season consisted of second and third place at Monza, obtained once again by Tambay and by Mario Andretti who, following an absence of 11 years, had returned to drive a Ferrari in the last two races of the season. The Maranello company took the Manufacturer's title, although this was poor consolation if one considered the potential that the team had shown.

In 1983, the regulations imposed the abolition of the miniskirts and the adoption of a flat bottom inside the car's wheelbase. The 126 C2 was therefore brought up to date, giving rise to the 126 C2/B, which was used until the Canadian Grand Prix with two victories to its credit: one gained by Tambay at Imola, and the other by Arnoux, the team's new member, at Montreal. The most significant innovations included the rear suspension with pullrod that appeared from the San Marino Grand Prix onward. The new 126 C3 made its debut in England, and was fitted with a monocoque entirely in carbon fiber and kevlar which, among other things, meant that the use of traditional bodywork could be limited to the sides, the nose, and the engine cowling. However, the sides, which had been tested in the wind tunnel with a markedly arrow-shaped conformation, proved to be inadequate and only the longer ones belonging to the C2B were used in races. Meanwhile, the power of the engine had increased to 600 hp at 10,500 rpm. Thanks to the two victories obtained by Arnoux at Hockenheim and Zandvoort, as well as numerous placings, the 126 C3 made a valid contribution to winning the Manufacturer's Championship, although Nelson Piquet took the driver's title with Brabham-BMW.

Technical data

MODEL 126 C2
YEAR OF PRODUCTION 1982

ENGINE
position: rear central longitudinal; **cylinders:** 120° 6V-cm^3 1,496; **feed:** 2 KKK turbocompressors - electronically operated Lucas-Ferrari injection; **ignition:** single; **timing:** 4 valves per cylinder-2 chain-driven OHC per cylinder bank; **max power:** 426 kW (580 hp) at 11,000 rpm.

CHASSIS
gearbox: 5-speed transverse + reverse; **suspensions:** front: wishbones, pullrod coil springs — rear: wishbones, pullrod, coil springs; **brakes:** front: self-ventilating discs — rear: self-ventilating discs; **wheelbase** (mm): 2,658.

Ferrari 126 C2

Ferrari F1/86

126 C4 / 156/85 / F1/86 / F1/87

In the 1984 126 C4 the engine was subjected to in depth revision, especially in light of the new rules which imposed a maximum consumption of 58 U.S.gals (220 liters) for each Grand Prix contest. It also abolished the practice of refuelling which had characterized the previous season. New heads and an entirely electronic injection system were adopted. The latter had two injectors per cylinder which, however, made way for the old Lucas mechanical system in some races. The position of the engine was also lowered and its weight was reduced by about 10%, while the Emulsystem tank, which had previously been separate, was incorporated in the driving seat. The power rose to 660 hp at 11,000 rpm, thanks also to the definitive adoption of modifications such as water cooling for the turbines. Starting with the Dutch Grand Prix, Ferrari was also able to exploit, as the 4-cylinder BMW had already done in the previous season, special heavy weight gasoline prepared by AgipPetroli.

The chassis bettered the layout of the C3 with its rigidity being increased and the weight further reduced, while as far as the brake system was concerned, the carbon discs made their debut. Lastly, the sidepods assumed the desired arrowshape design.

Ferrari's 1984 season will always be remembered as the last under the technical management of Mauro Forghieri, who was replaced by Harvey Postlethwaite after the Zandvoort trials. The first result produced by the new technical staff was the 126 C4/M2, which appeared for the first time at Monza with mechanics that were virtually unchanged, but with a longer wheelbase and completely redesigned aerodynamics, with lengthened sides and the tapering typical of the latter in front of the rear wheels which had been successfully introduced by McLaren and allowed for a better ratio between penetration and lift on the rear axle.

The season, which was dominated by the McLarens driven by Lauda and Prost, ended with Alboreto's only victory at Zolder. The Italian driver was also second at Monza and the Nürburgring, while Arnoux took second place at Imola and Dallas.

Numerous innovations were introduced to the single-seater designated 156/85 that was prepared for the 1985 season.

Arnoux, at the wheel of his 126 C4, during the 1984 San Marino Grand Prix.

Although the engine retained the basic 120° layout, it was modified by inverting the position of the feed, which was moved between the cylinder banks and the exhausts, which were now external and pointing downward. The improved Weber-Marelli electronic injection and a new design for the heads allowed 780 hp to be generated at 11,000 rpm, even after the Emulsystem had been abandoned, having been rendered superfluous by the quality of the gasoline used. As far as Ferrari was concerned, the season was divided into two distinct phases. In the first, Alboreto, now joined by Johansson, was able to compete on equal terms with McLaren for the conquest of the title. In fact, in his favor were four second places in Brazil, Portugal, Monaco, and England; two victories in Canada and Germany, as well as third place in Detroit and Zeltweg. In the second phase, which began with the Dutch Grand Prix, the 156 revealed notable problems regarding the engine's reliability (linked to the search for increasingly high power), followed by difficulties in the car's adjustment at high performance. The new version of the car which appeared at Monza with modifications to the chassis and the positioning of the cool-

In 1986, Alboreto was often forced to retire due to problems with the engine of his F1/86.

ing elements served no purpose. In the last six races, Alboreto did not manage to climb onto the podium once, leaving the path to the title free for Prost and his McLaren.

Following a year which ended in such a negative fashion, an intensive reorganization program of Ferrari's racing department began. Under the direction of engineer Tomaini, the technical staff now included such specialists such as Postlethwaite (for the chassis), the Frenchman Migeod (for the aerodynamics), and the ex-head of Renault engines, engineer His (who was charged with looking after the 120° 6-V engines). Under the new regulations the engines were allowed a maximum consumption of 51.5 U.S.gals (195 liters) per Grand Prix race. In order to remain within this limit without excessive sacrifices in terms of power, the combustion chambers were revised, as well as improvements made on the electronic operation of the injection and ignition. During the season, the Garrett turbines replaced the KKKs, while much work was done on the exhaust structure. The generated power was 850 hp at 11,500 rpm with a supercharged pressure of 3.6 bar. The rapid progress common to all the best turbo engines of the period soon meant that this value was increased to over 900 hp in the racing version.

The chassis of the new F1/86, once again built of carbon fiber and kevlar, was developed from scratch in a structure consisting of two parts: a single upper element that also included the sides to which the bottom was welded. The suspensions remained unchanged in their overall layout, and consisted of trailing arms fitted with aerodynamic fairings in carbon. In the rear a scheme with pull rods and almost horizontal dampers was adopted. In the French Grand Prix, a new front suspension was adopted, causing a slight increase in the wheelbase. However, the dimension of the latter was subject to frequent adaptations depending on whether a spacer flange between the engine and gearbox was adopted or not.

The phase of reorganizing the team, with renewed infrastructures, including a new wind tunnel (although this did not become functional until the end of the season), limited the team's expectations right from the start, and in fact the results were not outstanding. Of the two drivers, Alboreto and Johansson, it was the Swede who obtained the best placings, taking third place four times, in Belgium, Austria, Italy, and Australia, and fourth place twice, at Imola and in Hungary. As far as the Italian driver was concerned, he obtained a single second place in Austria, and two fourths and one fifth place, as well as a long series of withdrawals.

At the end of 1986, Ferrari hired John Barnard — the designer of the MP4 that had won the World Championship three times — away from McLaren, and he was charged with the task of developing the new single-seater with 12-cylinder in-line aspirated engine under the regulations that were to cancel supercharging from Formula One racing beginning in 1989.

In the meantime, under Postlethwaite's management, Brunner, the German chassis specialist, His, and Migeod had prepared the new F1/87, which contained important innovations. In fact, the engine had been completely renewed with the adoption of a 90° angle between the cylinder banks and a cast iron monoblock instead of one in light alloy. Penalized by the maximum supercharged pressure of 4 bar established by the sports authorities, this engine nevertheless succeeded in developing slightly more power than the previous version, with 880 hp at 11,500 rpm (declared at the beginning of the season).

In the early part of the championship, the new Ferrari did not prove to be lacking in faults. Until the 11th race of the 16 in program, the booty collected by Alboreto and Gerhard Berger did not exceed two third places, in the case of the Italian, and four third places in that of the Austrian. However, the continuous im-

The 6-V turbo of the F1/87 was substantially modified with the adoption, among other things, of a 90° angle between the cylinder banks.

In 1987, Gerhard Berger was particularly successful toward the end of the season, gaining victories in Japan and Australia.

provements carried out on the cars began to produce results starting with the Grand Prix in Portugal, where Berger arrived in second place. This proved that the F1/87 could now compete on equal terms with Williams-Honda, which had dominated the Formula One scene until then. The most exhilarating results were obtained in the last two Grand Prix, with Berger's outright victory in Japan and in Australia, where Alboreto completed the team's success with his own second place.

Technical data

| MODEL F1/86 |
| YEAR OF PRODUCTION 1986 |

ENGINE
position: rear central longitudinal; **cylinders:** 120° 6V-cm³ 1,496; **feed:** 2 KKK turbocompressors-Weber-Marelli electronic digital injection; **timing:** 4 valves per cylinder-2 chain-driven OHC per cylinder bank; **max power:** 625 kW (850 hp) at 11,500 rpm.

CHASSIS
gearbox: 5-speed transverse + reverse; **suspensions:** front: wishbones pullrod/coil springs — rear: wishbones pull rod/coil springs; **brakes:** front: self-ventilating discs — rear: self-ventilating discs; **wheelbase** (mm): 2,766.

CONTENTS